REEF
FISH
Identification

CARIBBEAN, BAHAMAS, SOUTH FLORIDA

Travel Edition

PAUL HUMANN
NED DELOACH

NEW WORLD PUBLICATIONS, INC.
Jacksonville, Florida U.S.A.

MW00993929

CREDITS

Photography Editor: Eric Riesch
Copy Editor: Ken Marks
Art Director: Michael O'Connell
Print Consultant: D'Print Pte Ltd, Singapore
First Edition ISBN 978-1-878348-45-6; Second Edition ISBN 978-1-878348-69-2
First Edition, 2011; Second Edition 2019, Second Printing 2023
Publisher: New World Publications, Inc., 1861 Cornell Road, Jacksonville, FL 32207, (904) 737-6558,
www.fishid.com, orders@fishid.com

PHOTO CREDITS

All species photographs in this book were taken underwater in their natural habitat. Many underwater photographers added their work to this collection. The authors appreciate their efforts and assistance in making this book as comprehensive as possible. They include: **Jim Abernethy**, 129bl; **Lad Akins**, 29br, 54mr, 73mr; **Mike Bacon**, 101tr; **Jayne Baker**, 91mr; **Dr. James Bohnsack**, 101mr; **Mike Bryant**, 122t, 127mr, 127b, back cover-bl; **Joyce and Frank Burek**, 22br; **Rosemond Clery**, 125tl; **Ken Deaver**, 51bl; **Carlos Estape**, 24br; **A&A Ferrari/SeaPics**, 20br; **Fred Good**, 96bl; **David Hall**, 124ml; **Howard Hall**, 129tr; **Wayne Hasson**, 130br; **Mike Kelly**, 82tl; **Michael Lawrence**, 55tl; **Larry Lipsky**, 91mr; **Louis Johnson**, 88br; **Ken Marks**, 24ml&mr, 50t, 65br, 104ml; 114tl; **Fred McConnaughey**, 32br; **George McGuire**, 100bl; **Scott Michael**, 90bl, 107tl, tr; **Christopher Newbert**, 20tr; **Fraizer Nivens**, 128mr; **Doug Perrine/SeaPics**, 28br, 109br, 120tr, 128ml, 129br, **Dr. John Randall**, 75tr&b, 85bl; **Eric Riesch**, 14tl, 15ml, 23b, 25bl, 31t&mr, 34tl&tr, 35tr, 40mr, 44l, 51m, 53t, 54t, 55bl, 57mr, 66tr, 69mr, 75tl, 96tl, 102ml, 104b, 108mr, 111mr, 119tr; **Mike Seale**, 106bl; **David Snyder**, 86br, 88mr; **Sipke Stapert**, 25ml; **Walt Stearns**, 79tr&br; **Guy Stevens/ Manta Trust**, 131m; **Graeme Teague**, 87tl, 101tl; **Louis Usie**, 101bl; **Jeff Utt**, 113br; **Peter Verhoog**, 128t; **James Watt/SeaPics**, 129tl; **Keri Wilk**, 66tr, 72br, 88bl, 119mr; **Dick Zingula**, 99br; all remaining photographs were taken by **Ned DeLoach** and **Paul Humann**.

Scientific Acknowledgments

Special recognition must be given to the numerous ichthyologists who gave freely of their time, advice and knowledge in confirming or providing identifications and supplemental information. Without their most generous assistance, the value of this book as a reference source would be greatly diminished. Every attempt has been made to keep this text and the identifications as accurate as possible; however, without doubt a few errors crept in, these are the authors' sole responsibility.

Ms. Rachel Arnold, University of Washington, Seattle, WA – Frogfishes

Dr. James Bohnsack, Rosenstiel School of Marine and Atomospheric Science, Univ. of Miami, FL – General

Dr. Margaret Bradbury, California Academy of Sciences, San Francisco, CA – Batfishes

Dr. José I. Castro, Mote Marine Laboratory, Sarasota, FL – Sharks

Dr. Ileana E. Clavijo, University of North Carolina, Wilmington, NC – Parrotfishes, Wrasses

Dr. Kendall Clements, University of Auckland, New Zealand – Chubs

Dr. Michael L. Domeier, Marine Conservation Science Institute, Fallbrook, CA – Sea Basses/Hamlets

Dr. William Eschmeyer, California Academy of Sciences, San Francisco, CA – Scorpionfishes

Mr. Brian Farm, Tanzania Wildlife Conservation Monitoring – Parrotfishes, Wrasses

Dr. David Greenfield, University of Hawaii, Honolulu, HI – Gobies, Blennies, Clingfishes, Cardinalfishes

Dr. Philip Hastings, Scripps Institution of Oceanography, La Jolla, CA – Blennies

Dr. Joseph Kimmel, National Marine Fisheries Service, St. Petersburg, FL – Sea Basses, General

Dr. Steen Knudsen, University of Auckland, New Zealand – Chubs

Mr. Mark Leiby, Florida Marine Research Institute, St. Petersburg, FL – Flounders

Dr. Ken Lindeman, Florida Institute of Technology, Melbourne, FL – Grunts, Snappers

Dr. Edward Matheson, Florida Marine Research Institute, St. Petersburg, FL – Mojarras

Dr. John McCosker, California Academy of Sciences, San Francisco, CA – Eels, General

Dr. Thomas Munroe, National Marine Fisheries Service, Washington, D.C. – Flatfishes

Dr. Jack Randall, Bishop Museum, Honolulu, HI – Surgeonfishes, Porgies, Blennies, General

Dr. Ross Robertson, Smithsonian Tropical Research Institute, Balboa, Panama – Dartfishes, Damselfishes

Dr. Richard Rosenblatt, Scripps Institution of Oceanography, La Jolla, CA – Triplefin Blennies

Dr. David G. Smith, Smithsonian, National Museum of Natural History, Suitland, MD – Eels

Dr. William Smith-Vaniz, U.S. Geological Survey, Gainesville, FL – Jacks, Jawfishes, General

Dr. Victor G. Springer, Smithsonian, National Museum of Natural History, Washington, D.C. – Blennies

Dr. Mark Steele, University of California, Santa Barbara, CA – Damselfishes

Dr. James Tyler, Smithsonian, National Museum of Natural History, Washington, D.C. – General

Dr. Benjamin C. Victor, CEO Ocean Science Foundation – Blennies, Gobies, General

Dr. Jeffrey T. Williams, Smithsonian, National Museum of Natural History, Suitland, MD – Blennies

Dr. Richard Winterbottom, Royal Ontario Museum, Toronto, Canada – Filefishes

Four ichthyologists listed above have been especially helpful and deserve additional comment.

Dr. William Smith-Vaniz was my wild dive buddy as we searched well below safe diving limits, at night and without lights, for the first living specimens of *Kryptophanaron alfredi* in 1977. Bill continues to be a friend and important source of information.

Dr. John McCosker is another madman who went well below safe limits with me to capture the second living specimens of *Kryptophanaron alfredi* – an expedition dubbed the "Krypto Caper." John and I continue our friendship and enjoy research expeditions together. He opened many doors to the scientific community.

Dr. James Bohnsack has become a friend and regular source of assistance and information. Many of his identification tips and methodology have been incorporated into this book. Jim's guidance, encouragement and influential status within the scientific community continues to be extremely valuable in the development of REEF (Reef Environmental Education Foundation).

Dr. Benjamin Victor has help us totally revise, improve and add numerous species to the goby and blenny sections of the book. Ben graciously assisted with several other families as well. Personally diving with someone as experienced and knowledgeable of fishes has been a rare pleasure.

Contents

How To Use This Book

Twelve Identification Groups

1. Disks & Ovals/Colorful   12-17

Angelfishes, pg. 13   Butterflyfishes, pg. 15   Surgeonfishes, pg. 17

2. Silvery   18-29

  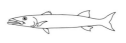 

Jacks, pg. 19   Mackerels, pg. 22   Barracudas, pg. 23   Tarpons, pg. 23

Needlefishes, pg. 24   Halfbeaks, pg. 24   Grunts, pg. 24   Mojarras, pg. 25

Porgies, pg. 26   Bonefishes, pg. 27   Snooks, pg. 27   Dolphinfishes, pg. 28

Chubs, pg. 28

Mullets, pg. 28

Spadefishes, pg. 28

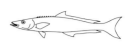
Cobias, pg. 29

3. Sloping Heads/Tapered Bodies

30-35

Grunts, pg. 31

Snappers, pg. 34

4. Small Ovals

36-43

Damselfishes, pg. 37

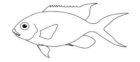
Chromis/Damselfishes, pg. 40

Hamlets/Sea Basses, pg. 42

5. Heavy Bodies/Large Lips

44-55

Groupers/Sea Basses, pg. 45

Basses/Sea Basses, pg. 50

Soapfishes/Sea Basses, pg. 54

Basslets, pg. 55

6. Swim with Pectoral Fins/Obvious Scales

56-69

Parrotfishes, pg. 57

Wrasses, pg. 62

Hogfishes/Wrasses, pg. 67

Razorfishes/Wrasses, pg. 68

7. Reddish/Big Eyes   70-76

Squirrelfishes, pg. 71

Bigeyes, pg. 72

Cardinalfishes, pg. 73

8. Small, Elongated Bottom-Dwellers   77-96

Gobies, pg. 78

Blennies, pg. 85

Dragonets, pg. 95

Jawfishes, pg. 96

9. Odd-Shaped Bottom Dwellers   97-109

Flounders, pg. 98

Clingfishes, pg. 100

Batfishes, pg. 100

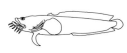

Toadfishes, pg. 101

Lionfishes, pg.102

Scorpionfishes, pg.102

Flying Gurnards, pg. 104

Searobins, pg. 104

Stargazers, pg. 104

Hawkfishes, pg. 104

Lizardfishes, pg. 105

Frogfishes, pg. 106

Seahorses, pg. 108

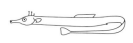

Pipefishes, pg. 109

10. Odd-Shaped Swimmers

Trumpetfishes, pg. 111

Cornetfishes, pg. 111

Puffers, pg. 112

Porcupinefishes, pg. 112

Boxfishes, pg. 114

Triggerfishes, pg. 115

Filefishes, pg. 116

Sweepers, pg. 118

Goatfishes, pg. 118

Tilefishes, pg. 118

Drums & Croakers, pg. 118

Brotulas, pg. 120

Tripletails, pg. 120

Remoras, pg. 120

11. Eels

121-125

Morays, pg. 122

Conger Eels/Garden Eels, pg. 124

Snake Eels, pg. 125

12. Sharks & Rays

126-131

Nurse Sharks, pg. 127

Pointed-Nose Sharks, pg. 127

Hammerheads, pg. 129

Rays, pg. 130

How To Use This Book

Identification Groups

Trying to identify a specific fish from the more than 500 species inhabiting the Tropical Western Atlantic can be a perplexing task. To help simplify the process, fish families with similar physical or behavioral characteristics have been arranged together into one of 12 color-coded and numbered ID Groups. This approach varies significantly from the traditional system that orders species chronologically by evolutionary development. Although there are a few anomalies, most families, genera and species integrate easily into this visually oriented system.

The ID Groups and their representative families are displayed on the Contents pages. Each group's similar characteristics are listed in italic type at the beginning of its ID Group. It is important for beginning fish watchers to become familiar with the major families that make up ID Groups, so they can go quickly to the correct section to begin the identification process. Families are scientific groupings based on evolutionary sequence and consequently, typically have similar physical characteristics. An overview of the family's behavioral and physical characteristics (that are observable by divers) is presented at the beginning of each ID Group.

Names

Information about each species begins with its common name (that generally used by the English speaking public). Common names are far from standardized and tend to vary from region to region, and on occasion within a region. For example, Mangrove Snapper and Gray Snapper refer to the same species. The American Fisheries Society has helped to standardize common names by publishing a preferred list that is updated every decade. Their recommendations are used in this book. Common names are capitalized in this text to help them stand apart from descriptive adjectives, although this practice is not considered grammatically correct.

To the right of a species' common name is the species' two-part scientific name, printed in italic. These names, rooted in Latin and Greek, are highly standardized and used by scientists throughout the world. The first word (always capitalized) represents the genus. The genus name is given to a group of species, which share a common ancestor, and usually have similar anatomical and physiological characteristics. The second word (never capitalized) is the species. A species includes only animals that are sexually compatible and produce fertile offspring. Each species usually, but not always, has a combination of visually distinctive features that separates them from all others.

The common and scientific family names follow. Because of its importance in the identification process, the common family name is also printed at the top of left pages where family members appear. Like common species names, common family names also vary between regions. In a few cases, when a distinctive group of fishes within a family are widely known by an alternative name, both names are included together separated by a slash.

The Use of Multiple Photographs for a Species

Several species are presented with more than one photograph. This is necessary to demonstrate differences in color, markings and physical features that occur within the same species. Such differences are primarily related to one of four categories:

Variations — Species, particularly those from different geographical regions, occasionally exhibit PERMANENT color or marking patterns or physical features distinctly different from the primary species illustrated.

Color and Marking Phases — Often a species may temporarily alter its color or markings, or physical features to inhance camouflage, indicate a change of mood, or for intraspecies communications, such as courtship. Phases can be changed instantaneously, or, in a few cases, over an extended period of time.

Life Cycle Phases — The juvenile forms (sexually immature individuals) of many species appear distinctly different from adults. These juveniles have been displayed, in most instances. However, no attempt has been made to include juveniles that resemble the adults, or that live in habitats not frequented by divers.

In the parrotfish and wrasse families life cycle phases are more complicated: besides juveniles, adults of most species display two visually distinct phases: the Initial Phase (IP), which generally includes both sexually mature males and females, and the Terminal Phase (TP), which includes only males, that are not only the least abundant, but the largest and most colorful individuals of the species.

Sexes — Males and females of many species display dissimilarity in colors or markings, or differences in body size, or the size and shape of anatomical features, such as fins.

Size

The general size range of the fish that divers are most likely to observe, followed by the species' maximum recorded size.

ID: Description

A species' account is given under the heading ID. Although the visual descriptions in this text might seem redundant to a species' image printed above, this information is often essential when features of an unidentified fish do not exactly match the photograph. In many cases a fish is so distinctive that making a comparison with its photograph easily substantiates its identification. However, because many genera include "similar-appearing" species the identification process is often more complex. Wherever similar-appearing species occur within a genus, every effort has been make to place the species together. Likewise, similar-appearing genera within a family, and similar families within an ID Group have been grouped whenever possible.

To help distinguish between similar-appearing species "distinctive features" that visually differentiate one species from the other have been highlighted with bold text, and where appropriate, an arrow pointing to the emphasized characteristic has been superimposed over the photograph.

In some cases the distinctive features emphasized are too small or subtle to establish reliable visual identifications with the naked eye underwater. However, this information, which includes such things as number of scale rows, spine counts, or nostril position, might be relied upon for making identifications from photographic images that can be enlarged and studied in detail.

Behavioral traits that may be observed by a diver and might help in the identification process are also listed under ID following the species' description. This brief information is usually coupled with a species' social organization: solitary, in pairs, form groups, or aggregations, followed by the species' habitat preference and depth range where it typically occurs.

Colors — The colors of many species vary considerably from individual to individual. In such situations, the description might read: "Reddish brown to olive-brown or gray." This means that the fish could be any of the colors or shades between. Many fishes also have an ability to pale, darken, and change colors. Because of this, color alone is rarely relied on for identification.

Range & Abundance

Range describes where the species is found in the Caribbean, Bahamas and South Florida. Often the range of a species extended beyond the area covered this book. This information has not been included in the text. Each geographical region is preceded by the species' relative abundance. If the abundance within this range varies, the locations are listed in sequence from regions of most sightings to those of least sightings.

Abundance refers to a diver's likelihood of observing a species in its normal habitat and depth range on any given dive. Because of reclusive habits and other factors, this does not always present an accurate portrait of actual populations. Definitions are as follows:

Abundant — Several sightings can be expected on nearly every dive.

Common — Sightings are frequent, but not necessarily expected on every dive.

Occasional — Sightings are not unusual, but are not expected on a regular basis.

Uncommon — Sightings are unusual.

Rare — Sightings are exceptional.

Not Reported — The species has not been reported from the indicated area.

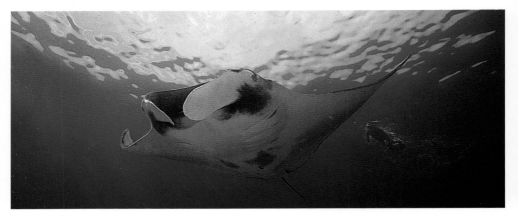

Markings

The terminology used to describe fish markings is defined in the following drawings.

STRIPE - Horizontal Marking

SPECKLES - Marked with fine spots

SPOT - circular marking

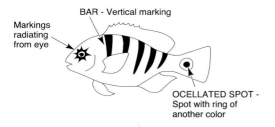

BAR - Vertical marking

Markings radiating from eye

OCELLATED SPOT - Spot with ring of another color

BAND - Diagonal marking

LINES - Thin markings of any orientation

BLOTCH - irregular marking

Anatomy

Anatomical features are often referred to as part of the identification process. The features used in this text are pinpointed in the following drawings

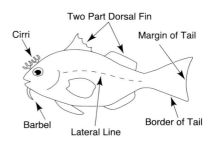

Cirri

Two Part Dorsal Fin

Margin of Tail

Barbel

Lateral Line

Border of Tail

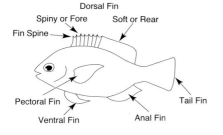

Dorsal Fin

Spiny or Fore   Soft or Rear

Fin Spine

Pectoral Fin

Ventral Fin   Anal Fin   Tail Fin

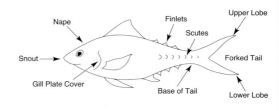

Nape

Finlets   Upper Lobe

Scutes

Snout

Gill Plate Cover

Base of Tail

Forked Tail

Lower Lobe

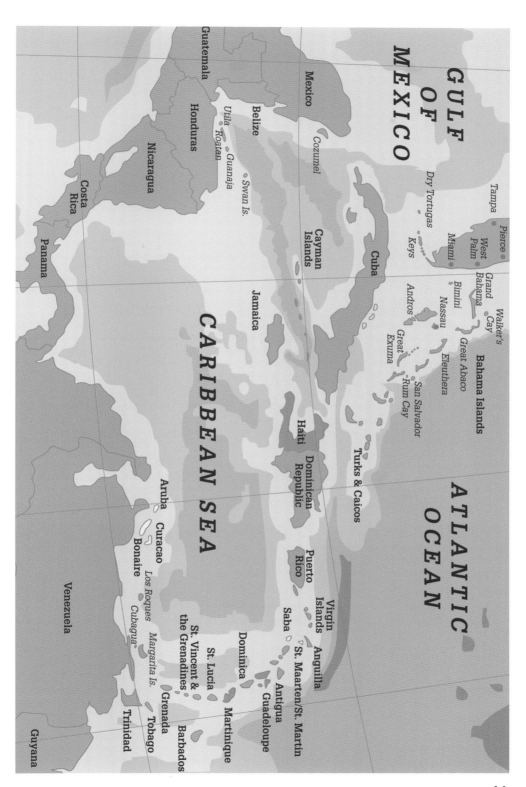

IDENTIFICATION GROUP 1

Disks & Ovals/Colorful
Angelfishes – Butterflyfishes – Surgeonfishes

This ID Group consists of fishes that are thin-bodied and have round or oval profiles. All have small mouths and are generally quite colorful.

Angelfishes
7 species, pg. 13

Butterflyfishes
5 species, pg. 15

Surgeonfishes
3 species, pg. 17

Angelfishes, Pomacanthidae – Beautiful, disk-shaped angelfishes are similar in shape and habitat preference to butterflyfishes; in fact, both groups were included in the same family for many years. Their flattened bodies, which make them difficult for predators to attack, allow the fishes to roam freely. Angelfishes swim more gracefully, and generally reach a length of a foot or more (exceptions are the Cherubfish and Flameback, which grow to only three inches). Unlike butterflyfishes, angelfishes have long, trailing dorsal and anal fins, and rounded foreheads. A spine extending from the rear cheek over the lower gill cover conclusively distinguishes angelfishes from butterflyfishes. Adult angelfishes are easily distinguished from one another; however, several juveniles are quite similar in both markings and color, making them more difficult to identify to species. The Queen and Blue Angelfishes, like the Gray and French Angelfishes, have similar body shapes and markings both as adults and juveniles; however, each has distinctive features that make underwater identification simple. The Cherubfish, primarily found on deeper reefs throughout the region, and the rare Flameback from the southeastern Caribbean, are the only family members that do not resemble the others in shape and size.

Butterflyfishes, Chaetodontidae – Reminiscent of their butterfly namesake, these small, colorful fishes flit about the reefs in search of food. They travel alone, or often in mated pairs, using keen eyesight to spot tiny worms and other marine invertebrates. These round, thin-bodied fishes are easy to recognize. Their small size (usually less than six inches) and slightly concave foreheads and lack of trailing dorsal and anal fins make them easy to distinguish from the larger angelfishes which have rounded foreheads and flowing fins. Butterflyfishes are silver to white, with yellow tints and dark markings. Dark eyebars on all butterflyfish and false eyespots on juveniles and two adults, are adaptations thought to confuse predators.

Surgeonfishes, Acanthuridae – A spine as sharp as a surgeon's scalpel, located on each side of the body at the base of the tail, is the origin of this family's common name. These formidable defensive weapons cannot be voluntarily erected; instead, the forward-pointing tips of the convex blades slip slightly from their grooves each time the tail flexes. Surgeonfishes are thin-bodied and oval, with long dorsal and anal fins, and a crescent tail. All are commonly sighted reef inhabitants that often mix in loose aggregations as they feed on algae. The Ocean Surgeonfish and Doctorfish are easy to confuse, but can be distinguished underwater by careful observation. Their juveniles are marked like the adults. Blue Tang are rounder, and usually seen in large groups; their juveniles are yellow.

QUEEN ANGELFISH *Holacanthus ciliaris*
SIZE: 8-14 in., max. 18 in. Angelfishes – Pomacanthidae
ID: Dark blue spot on forehead, speckled and ringed with blue, forms the "crown." Blue to greenish blue; yellow rims on scales; yellow tail, ventral and pectoral fins. **RANGE:** Common to occasional Caribbean, Bahamas, S. Florida.

Queen Angelfish – Juvenile **SIZE:** 1-5 in.
ID: Mid-body bars curved. Dark blue body with three blue to white bars; dark blue bar bordered in blue across eye; yellow lips; yellow area from around pectoral to ventral fins; yellow tail.

BLUE ANGELFISH *Holacanthus bermudensis*
SIZE: 8-14 in., max. 18 in. Angelfishes – Pomacanthidae
ID: Tail and pectoral fins bordered in yellow. Purplish to blue-green often with pronounced gray cast; rims of scales pale. Ventral fins yellow; dorsal and tail fins covered with yellowish to brown dots. **RANGE:** Common S. Florida, uncommon to rare Bahamas; rare Caribbean.

Blue Angelfish – Juvenile **SIZE:** 1-5 in.
ID: Mid-body bars straight, differentiates juvenile Blue Angelfish from juvenile Queen Angelfish [above].

ROCK BEAUTY *Holacanthus tricolor*
SIZE: 5-8 in., max. 12 in. Angelfishes – Pomacanthidae
ID: Yellow to yellow-orange forebody and tail; mid and rear body black. Face and lips occasionally navy blue. Individuals along North and South American coasts less brilliantly colored. **RANGE:** Common Caribbean; common to occasional Bahamas, S. Florida.

Rock Beauty – Juvenile **SIZE:** 1-2 in.
ID: Very young to two inches have a black spot ringed in brilliant blue on rear body. The blue ring is lost and the black spot increases in size with maturity until it covers the body.

FRENCH ANGELFISH *Pomacanthus paru*

SIZE: 10-14 in., max. 18 in. Angelfishes – Pomacanthidae

ID: Black with bright yellow rims on scales; tail rounded. Yellow ring around eye. All fins black except base of pectoral which is yellow. **RANGE:** Common to occasional Caribbean, Bahamas, S. Florida.

French Angelfish – Juvenile **SIZE:** 1-5 in.

ID: Rounded tail with yellow border forming an oval. (Differentiates juvenile French Angelfish from juvenile Gray Angelfish [below].) Black with three yellow body bars; yellow band extends down from forehead, stops at base of upper lip, splits and encircles mouth.

GRAY ANGELFISH *Pomacanthus arcuatus*

SIZE: 10-18 in., max. 2 ft. Angelfishes – Pomacanthidae

ID: Yellow inner face of pectoral fin. Light gray to grayish brown with light-edged dark scales. Swim about reefs, often in pairs. Easily approached. **RANGE:** Common to occasional Caribbean, Bahamas, S. Florida.

Gray Angelfish – Juvenile **SIZE:** 1-5 in.

ID: Tail has white to transparent margin. Black with three yellow bars on body and on on foretail. Yellow band extends down from forehead and across lips to chin; yellow ring around border of lips.

CHERUBFISH

Centropyge argi

Angelfishes – Pomacanthidae

SIZE: $1^1/_2$-$2^1/_2$ in., max. 3 in.

ID: Yellow to orange face and chest. (Similar Flameback [next] orange to yellow extends onto back and dorsal fin.) Dark blue body. Thin blue ring around eye; outer edge of dorsal and anal fins iridescent blue. **RANGE:** Common Cozumel, Bonaire, eastern Caribbean; occasional to rare remainder of Caribbean, Bahamas, S. Florida.

FLAMEBACK ANGELFISH
Centropyge aurantonotus
Angelfishes – Pomacanthidae
SIZE: 1 1/2-2 1/2 in., max. 3 in.
ID: Yellow to orange face and nape continuing onto back and dorsal fin. Dark blue body; orange on back extends to soft dorsal fin in young and recedes to spinous dorsal fin with age. Inhabit deep reefs and occasionally walls, usually deeper than 75 feet. Dart in and out of holes in rocks and coral. Swim in pairs or small groups, often mix with Cherubfish [previous]. **RANGE:** Occasional southeastern islands of Caribbean; absent balance of Caribbean, Bahamas, S. Florida.

BANDED BUTTERFLYFISH *Chaetodon striatus*
SIZE: 3-5 in., max. 6 in. Butterflyfishes – Chaetodontidae
ID: Two wide black midbody bars. Silver to white body; blackish border on rear of body, base of rear dorsal and anal fins. **RANGE:** Common to occasional Caribbean, Bahamas, S. Florida.

Banded Butterflyfish – Juvenile **SIZE:** 1 1/2 -3 in.
ID: Black spot ringed in white on rear dorsal fin. Easily distinguished from other butterflyfish juveniles by having no yellow on fins.

FOUREYE BUTTERFLYFISH *Chaetodon capistratus*
SIZE: 3-5 in., max. 6 in. Butterflyfishes – Chaetodontidae
ID: Black spot ringed in white on rear body near upper base of tail. Silver-gray body; marked with numerous dark, thin lines that radiate diagonally. **RANGE:** Abundant to common Caribbean, Bahamas, S. Florida.

Foureye Butterflyfish – Juvenile **SIZE:** 1 1/2 -3 in.
ID: Two wide, dusky body bars. **Very young have second, smaller black spot ringed in white on rear dorsal above larger spot.**

SPOTFIN BUTTERFLYFISH *Chaetodon ocellatus*
SIZE: 3-6 in., max. 8 in. Butterflyfishes – Chaetodontidae
ID: Black dot on outer edge of rear dorsal fin. Silver to white body. Fins (except pectoral) bright yellow. **RANGE:** Common to occasional Caribbean, Bahamas, S. Florida.

Spotfin Butterflyfish – Juvenile SIZE: 1½ -3 in.
ID: Irregular body bar extends to anal fin. Tail translucent.

REEF BUTTERFLYFISH *Chaetodon sedentarius*
SIZE: 3-4 in., max. 6 in. Butterflyfishes – Chaetodontidae
ID: Broad, dark barlike area on rear body, including the rear portions of dorsal and anal fins. Yellowish back and dorsal fin; silver-white lower body; yellowish tail. **RANGE:** Common to occasional eastern and southern Caribbean, S. Florida; uncommon Bahamas and remainder of Caribbean.

Reef Butterflyfish – Juvenile SIZE: 1½ -3 in.
ID: Black bar on rear anal fin and base of tail; very young have small black spot on rear dorsal fin.

LONGSNOUT BUTTERFLYFISH
Prognathodes aculeatus
Butterflyfishes – Chaetodontidae
SIZE: 2-3 in., max. 3½ in.
ID: Long pointed snout. Dusky to yellow bar runs from upper head across eye, but not below eye as in other butterflyfishes. Upper half of body yellowish changing to orange. Usually solitary and wary; generally inhabit deeper reefs and walls from 30 to 300 ft. Tend to be more secretive than other family members; use elongate mouth in deep recesses to feed on marine invertebrates. **RANGE:** Common to occasional Caribbean, Bahamas, S. Florida.

OCEAN SURGEONFISH *Acanthurus tractus*

SIZE: 6-12 in., max. 15 in. Surgeonfishes – Acanthuridae

ID: Uniform color with no body bars. Pectoral fin tissue clear, often with yellowish tint. Can change from bluish gray to dark brown, and pale or darken dramatically. May show white blotch on tail base. **RANGE:** Abundant to common Caribbean, Bahamas, S. Florida.

BLUE TANG
Acanthurus coeruleus

Surgeonfishes – Acanthuridae

SIZE: 5-10 in., max. 15 in.

ID: Yellow to white spine on base of tail. Can change from powder blue to deep purple, and pale or darken. Can be solitary, but more often in large aggregations foraging about shallow reef tops, grazing on algae. Aggregations may contain Ocean Surgeonfish, Doctorfish as well as fish predators attempting to conceal their presence. **RANGE:** Abundant to common Caribbean, Bahamas, S. Florida.

DOCTORFISH *Acanthurus chirurgus*

SIZE: 6-12 in., max. 14 in. Surgeonfishes – Acanthuridae

ID: Always display body bars (10-12), although they may be faint. Inner pectoral fin and leading edge dark to nearly black. Can change from bluish gray to dark brown, and pale or darken dramatically. May show white blotch on tail base. **RANGE:** Common Caribbean, Bahamas, S. Florida.

Blue Tang – Intermediate **SIZE:** 3$^1/_2$ -5 in.

ID: Pale to deep blue head and body with **yellow tail.** Changes from juvenile to intermediate and adult color phases do not depend on size, and occasionally a yellow-phase juvenile may be larger than some adults.

Blue Tang – Juvenile **SIZE:** 1$^1/_2$ -3 in.

ID: Solid yellow, with thin blue margins on dorsal and anal fins.

Silvery
Jacks – Mackerels – Barracudas – Others

This ID Group consists of fishes that are silver to gray in color and are generally unpatterned; however, several species have bluish, yellowish or greenish tints and occasional markings. All have forked tails.

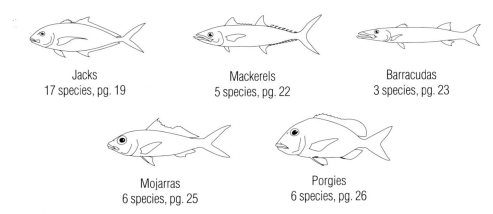

Jacks	Mackerels	Barracudas
17 species, pg. 19	5 species, pg. 22	3 species, pg. 23

Mojarras
6 species, pg. 25

Porgies
6 species, pg. 26

Jacks, Carangidae – Strong-swimming predators of the open sea, schools and solitary jacks occasionally pass over reefs in search of small fishes and crustaceans. Only a few species are seen about reefs on a regular basis. Most are thin, deep-bodied fish with small tail bases and deeply forked tails to facilitate speed.

Mackerels, Scombridae – These are long, silvery, strong, fast-swimming predators of the open sea that only occasionally pass over reefs. They have two dorsal fins that fold into grooves. A series of small fins, called finlets, are located on the back between the second dorsal fin and the tail, and also between the anal fin and the tail. The tail base is slender with two or more keels on each side.

Barracudas, Sphyraenidae – Because Great Barracudas, the most prominent member of the family, constantly work their tooth-lined jaws to help circulate water through their gills while stationary, these remarkable predators appear quite threatening. In actuality they pose little threat to divers. The few substantiated reports of attacks involved spearfishing or fish feeding. Unlike the Great Barracuda, which is typically solitary, the two smaller members of the family are usually sighted in small to large schools.

Mojarras, Gerreidae – These small, bright silver fishes with protrusible mouths and deeply forked tails inhabit shallow surge-swept sandy shorelines, and rubble, grass or mud flats where they feed on small, bottom-dwelling invertebrates. A few species are solitary, others form small schools. Although members of the family are easy to recognize as a group, distinguishing among several similar-appearing species is difficult in the field.

Porgies, Sparidae – Porgies are silvery fishes with high back profiles, large, steep heads, and mouths set well below the eyes. Their silvery color is often tinted with shades of blue and/or yellow, and many display head and/or body markings. Species are generally difficult to distinguish underwater, however, careful attention to detail usually makes identification possible. Juveniles are similar in appearance to adults. Porgies are solitary bottom feeders that dine on shellfish and crabs throughout the day.

BAR JACK *Caranx ruber*
SIZE: 8-14 in., max. 2 ft. Jacks – Carangidae
ID: **Bright blue and black border on back runs along dorsal fin and onto lower tail fin.** Silvery but can darken almost to black, especially when feeding near bottom. Swim in open water over reefs in small groups to large schools; also solitary. **RANGE:** Common Caribbean, Bahamas, S. Florida.

YELLOW JACK *Caranx bartholomaei*
SIZE: 1-2 ft., max. 3 ft. Jacks – Carangidae
ID: **Yellow lower tail fin.** Silvery, to yellow cast. Usually solitary or in small groups over outer reefs. **RANGE:** Occasional to uncommon Caribbean, Bahamas, S. Florida.

BLUE RUNNER *Caranx crysos*
SIZE: 1-2 ft., max. 2¹/₂ ft. Jacks – Carangidae
ID: **Tips of tail fin dark.** Bluish silver to brassy or olive. Somewhat elongate black spot near upper end of gill cover; may have faint bluish bars on body. Breeding males become blackish. **RANGE:** Occasional Bahamas, S. Florida; uncommon to rare Caribbean, except common along coast of Venezuela.

HORSE-EYE JACK *Caranx latus*
SIZE: 1-2 ft., max. 2¹/₂ ft. Jacks – Carangidae
ID: **Large eye.** Bright silver with yellow tail and nearly black scutes. usually have dark tips on dorsal and upper tail fin; often a small black spot at upper end of gill cover; may have darkish smudge on pectoral fin. **RANGE:** Common to occasional Caribbean, Bahamas, S. Florida.

CREVALLY JACK *Caranx hippos*
SIZE: 1-2 ft., max. 4 ft. Jacks – Carangidae
ID: **Blackish blotch on pectoral fin.** Grayish silver with black spot near top of gill cover. Tail and anal fin may be yellowish; tips of dorsal and upper tail occasionally black; scutes grayish. Eye small and steep head profile. Openwater species. **RANGE:** Uncommon to rare Caribbean, Bahamas, S. Florida.

BLACK JACK *Caranx lugubris*
SIZE: 1-2 ft., max. 3 ft. Jacks – Carangidae
ID: **Forehead (nape) steep.** Dark gray or brown to black, often with silvery to olive sheen. Small black spot on upper start of gill cover. Black dorsal, anal and tail fins, and scutes. Inhabit open water along outer reefs and walls and near deeper wrecks. **RANGE:** Uncommon to rare Caribbean, Bahamas, S. Florida.

19

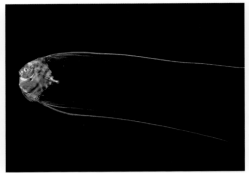

AFRICAN POMPANO *Alectis ciliaris*
SIZE: 1-2 ft., max. 3½ ft. Jacks – Carangidae
ID: Deep body with steep, blunt forehead. Often have bluish or greenish tints; scales not obvious. Compressed body, deeply forked tail. Openwater species. **RANGE:** Uncommon Caribbean, Bahamas, S. Florida.

African Pompano – Juvenile **SIZE:** 1-5 in.
ID: Diamond-shaped juveniles trail long threadlike filaments from dorsal and anal fins; as fish mature, filaments usually become progressively shorter, often completely disappearing in larger adults.

PERMIT *Trachinotus falcatus*
SIZE: 1-3 ft., max. 4 ft. Jacks – Carangidae
ID: Pectoral, tail and tips of anal dorsal fins dark. Brilliantly silver; often have tint of iridescent blue on head and back. Occasionally display a dark circular blotch behind base of pectoral fin. **RANGE:** Uncommon Caribbean, Bahamas, S. Florida.

PALOMETA *Trachinotus goodei*
SIZE: 7-13 in., max. 18 in. Jacks – Carangidae
ID: Extremely long dorsal, anal and tail fins edged in black. Silvery deep body with four body bars. School in shallow water often in surge. **RANGE:** Occasional eastern and southern Caribbean; uncommon to rare Bahamas, S. Florida and remainder of Caribbean.

LOOKDOWN *Selene vomer*
SIZE: 6-10 in., max. 1 ft. Jacks – Carangidae
ID: Very thin body with extremely blunt head. Bright silver, occasionally goldish, greenish, bluish or purplish highlights. May display three or four pale body bars. Fore part of dorsal and anal fins elongate. Prefer shallow often murky water. **RANGE:** Uncommon to rare Caribbean, Bahamas, S. Florida.

PILOTFISH *Naucrates ductor*
SIZE: 6-15 in., max. 2 ft. Jacks – Carangidae
ID: Five to seven bold dark bars encircle body. Silvery white to gray, torpedo-shaped body and forked tail. Accompany large fish, including sharks, rays, whales and occasionally ships. **RANGE:** Occasional Caribbean, Bahamas, S. Florida.

ALMACO JACK *Seriola rivoliana*
SIZE: 1-2 ft., max. 3 ft. Jacks – Carangidae
ID: Dark diagonal band runs from lip, across eye to beginning of dorsal fin. Silvery to dark gray with dusky fins and elongate foredorsal fin. Openwater species rarely over reef. Solitary or form small, loose schools. **RANGE:** Uncommon to rare Caribbean, Bahamas, S. Florida.

GREATER AMBERJACK *Seriola dumerili*
SIZE: 2-4 ft., max. 5½ ft. Jacks – Carangidae
ID: Diagonal band runs from lip, across eye to nape. Sleek, elongate body with short foredorsal fin. Silvery; fins may have yellow cast. Often display diffuse, yellowish or amber stripe along midbody. Openwater species seldom over reefs. **RANGE:** Uncommon Caribbean, Bahamas, S. Florida.

RAINBOW RUNNER *Elagatis bipinnulata*
SIZE: 2-3 ft., max. 4 ft. Jacks – Carangidae
ID: Two blue stripes run length of body with pale to brilliant yellow or gold stripe between. Silvery yellow to blue; tail fin yellowish. Head more pointed and body more elongate compared to most jacks. **RANGE:** Uncommon to rare Caribbean, Bahamas, S. Florida.

ROUND SCAD *Decapterus punctatus*
SIZE: 6-8 in., max. 10 in. Jacks – Carangidae
ID: Series of widely spaced small black spots along forward half of lateral line. Slender and elongate; bright reflective silver, occasionally with greenish sheen. Enlarged scutes on base of tail. Form large, rapidly swimming schools. **RANGE:** Occasional Caribbean, Bahamas, S. Florida.

MACKEREL SCAD *Decapterus macarellus*
SIZE: 6-10 in., max. 1 ft. Jacks – Carangidae
ID: Black spot at upper edge of gill plate. Bright, reflective silver elongate body often with bluish or greenish sheen. Occasionally display yellow midbody stripe; lateral line slightly arched. Form large, rapidly swimming schools. **RANGE:** Occasional Caribbean, Bahamas; uncommon S. Florida.

BIGEYE SCAD *Selar crumenophthalmus*
SIZE: 6-12 in., max. 2 ft. Jacks – Carangidae
ID: Large eye (diameter greater than snout length). Bright reflective silver with deeply forked tail; scutes only on rear lateral line. Form large, rapidly swimming schools. **RANGE:** Occasional to uncommon Caribbean, Bahamas, S. Florida.

CERO
Scomberomorus regalis
Mackerels – Scombridae
SIZE: 1½-3 ft., max. 4 ft.

ID: Series of yellow-gold streaks along midline from pectoral fin to tail. Silvery elongate body with small yellow-gold body spots on either side of streaks. Lateral line slopes gently downward below second dorsal fin. Openwater species usually solitary over deep reefs and drop-offs. **RANGE:** Occasional Caribbean, Bahamas, S. Florida.

SPANISH MACKEREL   *Scomberomorus maculatus*
SIZE: 1½-3 ft., max. 4 ft.   Mackerels – Scombridae
ID: Yellow-gold spots on sides. Silvery, elongate openwater species; back often darker with bluish or olive tint. Lateral line slopes gently downward below second dorsal fin. **RANGE:** Occasional S. Florida; rare to absent Caribbean, Bahamas.

KING MACKEREL   *Scomberomorus cavalla*
SIZE: 2-4 ft., max 5½ ft.   Mackerels – Scombridae
ID: Lateral line drops abruptly below second dorsal fin. Silvery, elongate openwater species with no markings; back often darker with bluish or olive cast. Solitary or small groups. Juveniles have small dark to gold spots on sides. **RANGE:** Rare Caribbean, Bahamas, S. Florida.

WAHOO   *Acanthocybium solandri*
SIZE: 4-5 ft., max. 7 ft.   Mackerels – Scombridae
ID: Sharply pointed snout. Long, bright silver to silvery gray cigar-shaped openwater species; back may have dark bluish cast. May display numerous dark bars, especially when stressed. Nine dorsal finlets and widely forked tail. **RANGE:** Uncommon Caribbean, Bahamas, S. Florida.

LITTLE TUNNY   *Euthynnus alletteratus*
SIZE: 2-3½ ft., max. 4 ft.   Mackerels – Scombridae
ID: Diagonal or wavy bands on back. Silvery openwater species with several dark spots below pectoral fins. Usually form loose schools; often over deep wrecks. **RANGE:** Uncommon Caribbean, Bahamas, S. Florida.

GREAT BARRACUDA
Sphyraena barracuda
Barracudas – Sphyraenidae
SIZE: 1¹/₂-3 ft., max. 6 ft.

ID: Large underslung jaw, pointed teeth often obvious. Long, cylindrical body usually with scattered, dark blotches. Can darken, showing side bands. Dorsal fins widely separated. Usually solitary but can form small groups. Curious; have the unnerving habit of approaching divers and following them, opening and closing mouth to assist respiration. Rarely known to attack divers. **RANGE:** Common to occasional Caribbean, Bahamas, S. Florida.

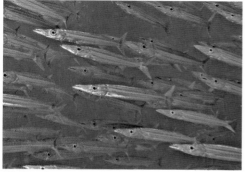

NORTHERN/SOUTHERN SENNET   *Sphyraena borealis/picudilla*
SIZE: 8-14 in., max. 18 in.   Barracudas – Sphyraenidae

ID: Long, slender and silver schooling fish with no obvious markings. (Similar Great Barracuda [previous] is heavier bodied and usually shows some dark markings.) May have two faint yellowish body stripes. Widely separated dorsal fins. **RANGE:** Uncommon Caribbean, Bahamas, S. Florida.

GUAGUANCHE   *Sphyraena guachancho*
SIZE: 6-14 in., max. 2 ft.   Barracudas – Sphyraenidae

ID: Yellowish to yellow or gold midbody stripe. Long, slender and silvery; back silvery brown to olive. Widely separated dorsal fins. **RANGE:** Uncommon Caribbean, Bahamas, S. Florida.

TARPON
Megalops atlanticus
Tarpons – Megalopidae
SIZE: 2-4 ft., max. 8 ft.

ID: Large, upturned mouth. Shiny, large "stainless steel" scales and stout body with no markings. Long filament trails from rear base of dorsal fin. Occasionally drift in schools in canyons and secluded areas during the day. Often solitary. Feed at night. **RANGE:** Occasional to uncommon Caribbean, Bahamas, S. Florida.

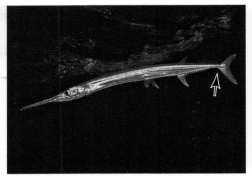

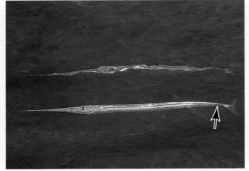

HOUNDFISH *Tylosurus crocodilus*
SIZE: 2-3½ ft., max. 5 ft. Needlefishes – Belonidae
ID: Black lateral keel on each side of tail base. Silver, elongate "needlelike" body. Beak short compared to most needlefishes, about one and a half times length of head; lower lobe of tail larger than upper. **RANGE:** Occasional Caribbean, Bahamas, S. Florida.

KEELTAIL NEEDLEFISH *Platybelone argalus*
SIZE: 10-15 in., max. 20 in. Needlefishes – Belonidae
ID: Wide, flattened, lateral keel on each side of tail base. Silver, elongate "needlelike" body. Beak long and slender, upper jaw slightly shorter than lower; lobes of tail nearly equal in size. **RANGE:** Occasional to uncommon Caribbean, Bahamas, S. Florida.

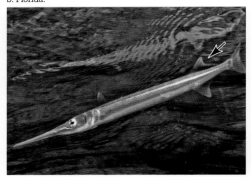

FLAT NEEDLEFISH *Ablennes hians*
SIZE: 1½-3 ft., max. 3½ ft. Needlefishes – Belonidae
ID: Numerous dark bars on body and dusky to black area on rear dorsal fin; Silvery elongate body with short beak about length of head, lower lobe of tail larger. **RANGE:** Occasional Florida, Bahamas, Caribbean.

REDFIN NEEDLEFISH *Strongylura notata*
SIZE: 1½-3 ft., max. 3½ ft. Needlefishes – Belonidae
ID: Areas of red to yellow on dorsal, tail and anal fins, and black bar on gill cover. Silvery elongate body with long beak that is often yellowish. **RANGE:** Occasional Florida, Bahamas, Caribbean.

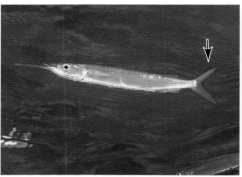

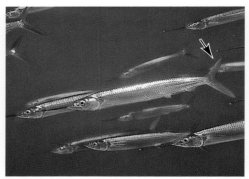

BALLYHOO *Hemiramphus brasiliensis*
SIZE: 8-12 in., max. 16 in. Halfbeaks – Hemiramphidae
ID: Upper lobe of tail yellow to orange. Silver; back often has greenish sheen. Upper jaw extremely short, lower jaw long with yellow to orange or red tip. Leading edge of dorsal fin often yellow to orange. Tail deeply forked; lower lobe largest. **RANGE:** Occasional Caribbean, Bahamas, S. Florida.

BALAO *Hemiramphus balao*
SIZE: 8-12 in., max. 15 in. Halfbeaks – Hemiramphidae
ID: Lobes of tail violet to blue. Silver, often with violet to blue sheen, especially on back. Upper jaw extremely short, lower jaw long with orange to red tip. Leading edge of dorsal fin often blue. Tail deeply forked; lower lobe largest. **RANGE:** Occasional to uncommon Caribbean, Bahamas, S. Florida.

YELLOWFIN MOJARRA *Gerres cinereus*
SIZE: 8-12 in., max. 16 in. Mojarras – Gerreidae
ID: Yellow ventral fins. Bright silver often with several indistinct vertical bars on body. Swim and hover over sand near reefs, stopping occasionally to dig for small invertebrates. **RANGE:** Common to occasional Caribbean, S. Florida; uncommon Bahamas.

FLAGFIN MOJARRA *Eucinostomus melanopterus*
SIZE: 4-6 in., max. 7 in. Mojarras – Gerreidae
ID: Spinous dorsal fin has black tip with white stripe below. Bright silver; back may have greenish or brownish tint. Often inhabit surge zones of beaches. **RANGE:** Uncommon Caribbean, S. Florida; rare Bahamas.

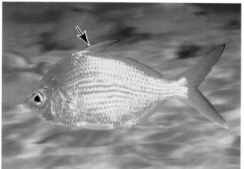

IRISH POMPANO *Diapterus auratus*
SIZE: 4-8 in., max. 1 ft. Mojarras – Gerreidae
ID: Spinous dorsal fin edged in black; second spine long and stout. Silvery with greenish tints on back; occasionally have purplish reflections. **RANGE:** Uncommon Caribbean, S. Florida; rare Bahamas.

SLENDER MOJARRA *Eucinostomus jonesii*
SIZE: 4-6 in., max. 8 in. Mojarras – Gerreidae
ID: Bright silver, slender body without other markings, but occasionally may display some dusky bars or mottling on back. May have dusky oval marking in front upper part of iris. **RANGE:** Occasional to uncommon Caribbean, Bahamas, S. Florida.

MOTTLED MOJARRA *Eucinostomus lefroyi*
SIZE: 4-7 in., max. 9 in. Mojarras – Gerreidae
ID: Dusky rectangular to roundish spot on central upper iris. Bright silver body, usually with some dusky bars or mottling on back. Foredorsal and tail fins often dusky and/or with darkish borders. **RANGE:** Occasional Caribbean, Bahamas, S. Florida.

SILVER JENNY *Eucinostomus gula*
SIZE: 3-5 in., max. 7 in. Mojarras – Gerreidae
ID: Usually have dusky tip on dorsal fin. Deep bright silver body; may have dusky diagonal bands or blotches on sides, especially when young. **RANGE:** Occasional to uncommon Caribbean, Bahamas, S. Florida.

SAUCEREYE PORGY   *Calamus calamus*
SIZE: 8-14 in., max. 16 in.   Porgies – Sparidae
ID: Short, bluish saucer-shaped line below eye. Silvery with bluish, yellowish and/or brassy cast. Small, bluish blotch at upper base of pectoral fin. Corners of mouth yellow. Swim and hover above reefs and adjacent sand areas. **RANGE:** Common to occasional Caribbean, Bahamas, S. Florida.

Saucereye Porgy – Phase
ID: Often yellow wash over head and forebody. Can change coloration rapidly and show a striped or blotched pattern, especially when feeding.

SHEEPSHEAD PORGY   *Calamus penna*
SIZE: 8-14 in., max. 18 in.   Porgies – Sparidae
ID: Black spot on upper base of pectoral fin. Silvery with bluish, lavender or yellow iridescent sheen. Usually pale gray or blue line around underside of eye. Upper jaw overbite. Swim and hover above reefs and adjacent sand areas. **RANGE:** Occasional S. Florida; uncommon to rare Caribbean, Bahamas.

Sheepshead Porgy – Phase
ID: Often display dark body bars when near bottom, especially when feeding; occasionally have dark margin on tail.

PLUMA PORGY   *Calamus pennatula*
SIZE: 8-12 in., max. 15 in.   Porgies – Sparidae
ID: Short, blue rectangular stripe behind eye. Silvery; commonly with yellow and/or brassy cast; nape and back often yellow. Bluish and brassy irregular lines and markings below eye. Can change colors rapidly. **RANGE:** Occasional to rare Caribbean, Bahamas; not reported S. Florida.

JOLTHEAD PORGY   *Calamus bajonado*
SIZE: 1-1½ ft., max. 2½ ft.   Porgies – Sparidae
ID: Large eye, long sloping snout and large mouth with thick lips. Stocky silver body; may have faint iridescent blue, blue-green, lavender and/or brassy cast. Usually two large, silvery, horizontal markings under eye and on gill cover. **RANGE:** Occasional Caribbean, Bahamas; rare S. Florida.

SILVER PORGY   *Diplodus argenteus*
SIZE: 4-8 in., max. 12 in.   Porgies – Sparidae
ID: Black spot on upper base of tail occasionally forming saddle over top. Silvery with thin, pale yellow stripes along scale rows. Ventral fins bluish silver, other fins yellowish. Occasionally have faint dusky vertical bars on body. **RANGE:** Uncommon S. Florida; rare Caribbean, Bahamas.

SEA BREAM   *Archosargus rhomboidalis*
SIZE: 5-8 in., max. 13 in.   Porgies – Sparidae
ID: Large dusky spot behind gill cover and below lateral line. Bluish silver with narrow yellow-gold stripes on body; ventral and anal fins orangish. Inhabit grass beds and mangroves. **RANGE:** Occasional to uncommon Caribbean, Florida; not reported Bahamas.

BONEFISH
Albula vulpes

Bonefishes – Albulidae
SIZE: 1-2$^{1}/_{2}$ ft., max. 3$^{1}/_{4}$ ft.

ID: Short, underslung mouth that ends before eye. Silver with numerous thin, dark scale stripes; darkish area at tip of snout and base of pectoral fin; may display faint bars; single dorsal fin and deeply forked tail. Feed over shallow flats on a rising tide, often near mangroves. When not feeding may be observed on sand and coral rubble flats near shallow patch reefs. **RANGE:** Occasional to uncommon Caribbean, Bahamas, S. Florida.

COMMON SNOOK
Centropomus undecimalis

Snooks – Centropomidae
SIZE: 1$^{1}/_{2}$-3$^{1}/_{2}$ ft., max. 4$^{1}/_{2}$ ft.

ID: Obvious black lateral line. Silvery olive with depressed forehead. Small groups often hover in secluded areas near mangroves or occasionally over grassy flats and shallow patch reefs. **RANGE:** Occasional Florida, and continental coasts of Central and northern South America; rare or absent Bahamas and islands of Caribbean.

DOLPHINFISH *Coryphaena hippurus*

SIZE: 2-4 ft., max. 5¼ ft. Dolphinfishes – Coryphaenidae
ID: Long, continuous dorsal fin extends from above eye to base of tail. Males with blunt heads display bright yellow, yellow-green and blue iridescent spots and washes. Also commonly known as "Mahi Mahi." **RANGE:** Common Florida, Bahamas; occasional Caribbean.

Dolphinfish – Female **SIZE:** 2-4 ft., max. 4½ ft.

ID: Rounded, torpedo-shaped heads display brilliant blue iridescence and washes with blue markings on head. Openwater species, often under *Sargassum* floats, rarely on shallow reefs. Usually in small aggregations of one or two bulls and numerous females.

CHUB (BERMUDA/GRAY)
Kyphosus sectatrix/bigibus
Sea Chubs – Kyphosidae
SIZE: 1-2 ft., max. 2½ ft.

ID: "Football-shaped" body. (Distinguishing between these two similar-appearing species underwater is virtually impossible — fin ray and gill raker counts are required to confirm identification.) Appear uniformly gray to silver; occasionally display whitish blotches. A close observation reveals thin yellow to bronze stripes on body and a stripe, bordered in white, under eye from mouth to gill cover. **RANGE:** Common to occasional Caribbean, Bahamas, S. Florida.

WHITE MULLET *Mugil curema*
SIZE: 8-12 in., max. 15 in. Mullets – Mugilidae
ID: Large, dusky to bluish black, semicircular or oval spot on base of pectoral fin. Silvery with obvious scales and dark to dusky margin on tip of rear dorsal fin and tail. Often have one or two goldish blotches on each side of head. **RANGE:** Occasional Caribbean, Bahamas, S. Florida.

STRIPED MULLET *Mugil cephalus*
SIZE: 1-2 ft., max. 3 ft. Mullets – Mugilidae
ID: Dark spots on base of each scale form stripes on side. Silvery, often with greenish, bluish or brownish tints; back appears dark because of large spot on each scale; belly silvery white; second dorsal fin and tail dusky. **RANGE:** Occasional S. Florida; rare to absent Caribbean, Bahamas.

ATLANTIC SPADEFISH
Chaetodipterus faber
Spadefishes – Ephippidae
SIZE: 1-1¹/₂ ft., max. 3 ft.

ID: Deep disc-shaped body **with several dark bars.** Silver may turn gray. Bars can pale dramatically. Body shape resembles a "spade" on playing cards. Usually in small schools in open water. **RANGE:** Common Bahamas, S. Florida; occasional Caribbean.

COBIA   *Rachycentron canadum*
SIZE: 2-4 ft., max. 6 ft.   Cobias – Rachycentridae

ID: Long "torpedo-shaped" body with flattened forebody. Silver to dark brown. Often have dusky midbody stripe. Lower jaw protrudes; tail forked. Coastal to openwater species; often hover below anchored ships and buoys. **RANGE:** Occasional S. Florida; uncommon to rare Caribbean, Bahamas.

BARBU   *Polydactylus virginicus*
SIZE: 4-8 in., max. 12 in.   Threadfins – Polynemidae

ID: Silvery with no distinctive markings. **Lower segment of two-part pectoral fin formed by long unconnected, filamentous rays.** Upper pectoral and ventral fins pale with darkish centers and white borders. **RANGE:** Occasional Caribbean, S. Florida; not reported Bahamas.

REDEAR HERRING   *Harengula humeralis*
SIZE: 3-6 in., max. 8 in.   Herrings – Clupeidae

ID: Red to yellow spot on upper end of gill cover. Silvery with darkish spots on scales forming thin dotted stripes on body; snout and lower jaw often orange-yellow. Form polarized schools in shallow bays and coastal waters. **RANGE:** Occasional Caribbean, Bahamas, S. Florida.

SILVERSIDES, HERRINGS, ANCHOVIES
SIZE: 1-3 in., max. 6 in.   Atherinidae, Clupeidae, Engraulididae

ID: Tiny silver, fork-tailed schooling fish. There are about 10 species of small, silver similar-appearing fishes that are difficult to distinguish underwater. Species often mix to form dense aggregations in cave and wreck entrances. **RANGE:** Occasional Caribbean, Bahamas, S. Florida.

Sloping Heads/Tapered Bodies
Grunts – Snappers

This ID Group consists of fishes that have what can best be described as a basic, "fishlike" shape, relatively large mouths and notched tails.

Grunts
15 species, pg. 31

Snappers
8 species, pg. 34

Grunts, Haemulidae – Grunts are closely related and similar in appearance to snappers, but are generally smaller (normally between 12 and 18 inches), with more deeply notched tails. They also lack the snappers' sharp canine teeth. Most are colorful, and congregate to rest during the day in small groups to large schools that drift in the shadows of reefs. At night, the nocturnal carnivores scavenge sand flats and grass beds for crustaceans. Grunts often make up the largest biomass on reefs in continental or insular shelf areas that have large expanses of seagrass beds and sand flats. Grunt populations are less prominent around islands lacking expansive shallow shelfs for seagrass meadows. The common family name is derived from the unusual "grunt" sound produced by flattened teeth plates grinding deep within the throats, which is amplified by the air bladder.

Differences in color, body stripes and tail markings are keys to species identification. Adults all have distinctive features and are fairly easy to distinguish. Those which may cause confusion are the Bluestripe and White Grunts; the Sailor's Choice and Black Grunt; and the more elongate Smallmouth and Striped Grunts. Identifying early juvenile grunts (one to two inches) is quite difficult. Most are silver-white with similar dark body stripes, and have a dot on the tail base. Careful attention to subtle differences, however, makes identification possible. Although Margate (white), Black Margate and Porkfish have higher back profiles and are somewhat larger the three species also belong to the family.

Snappers, Lutjanidae – Snappers are medium-sized (usually one to two feet), oblong-shaped fishes with triangular heads. All have a single, continuous dorsal fin that is often higher in the front, and shallow, notched tail. They have slightly upturned snouts, large mouths, and most species have prominent canine teeth near the front of the jaw. The behavior of snapping their jaws when hooked gives family members their common name. Snappers are nocturnal predators that feed on crustaceans and small fishes.

When seen on the reef in daytime, Dog, Cubera and Mutton Snappers tend to be solitary; Mahogany, Gray and Lane Snappers often gather in small mixed schools with grunts; Yellowtail Snappers swim in loose aggregations well above the reefs, but also feed in the sand, often joining mixed bottom-feeding aggregations; nocturnal Schoolmasters typically gather in schools during the day, although larger individuals may be solitary.

Dog, Cubera and Gray Snappers are difficult to differentiate, because of the similar body shapes and gray coloration, and only vague markings. Subtle differences between all these species, however, make underwater identification possible. Unlike larger adults, young Gray Snapper, that typically inhabit mangrove forests and shallow shore reefs, display dark eye bars.

BLUESTRIPED GRUNT
Haemulon sciurus
Grunts – Haemulidae
SIZE: 8-14 in., max. 18 in.
ID: Dark tail and rear dorsal fin. Blue stripes over yellow-gold. Dark tail and dorsal fins have light margins; other fins yellow. Congregate in small to midsized schools near protective reefs and drop-offs; larger individuals may be solitary. **RANGE:** Common to occasional Caribbean, Bahamas, S. Florida.

FRENCH GRUNT   *Haemulon flavolineatum*
SIZE: 6-10 in., max. 1 ft.   Grunts – Haemulidae
ID: Yellow stripes below lateral line set on diagonal. Yellow stripes on a white to bluish or yellowish silver background. Stripes above lateral line are horizontal. Fins yellow. **RANGE:** Abundant to common S. Florida; common to occasional Caribbean, Bahamas.

SMALLMOUTH GRUNT   *Haemulon chrysargyreum*
SIZE: 7-9 in., max. 10 in.   Grunts – Haemulidae
ID: Five or six yellow stripes. Stripes over bluish silver to silvery-white background. Have pale phase. Noticeably smaller mouth than other grunts. **RANGE:** Abundant to occasional Caribbean, S. Florida; uncommon Bahamas.

WHITE GRUNT   *Haemulon plumierii*
SIZE: 8-14 in., max. 18 in.   Grunts – Haemulidae
ID: Stripes only on head. Head stripes yellow and bluish silver. Large scales on upper body form checkered pattern of yellow and bluish silver, often with a pearly iridescence. Drift in small to large schools in shallow patch reefs or in shade of formations. **RANGE:** Common Caribbean, Bahamas, S. Florida.

CAESAR GRUNT   *Haemulon carbonarium*
SIZE: 7-12 in., max. 15 in.   Grunts – Haemulidae
ID: Yellow to dark copper/bronze stripes. Stripes over white to silver-blue or silver-gray background. Tail has pale margin. Dusky rear dorsal, anal and tail fins. **RANGE:** Common central and southeastern Caribbean, S. Florida; Uncommon northwest Caribbean and Bahamas..

Grunts

SAILORS CHOICE   *Haemulon parra*
SIZE: 8-12 in., max. 17 in.   Grunts – Haemulidae
ID: Black spots on scales form numerous oblique stripes on body. Silvery to pearly gray. Fins dusky to dark (except pectoral which may be light). Large eye with golden tint outside white iris. **RANGE:** Occasional Bahamas, S. Florida, and coasts of Central and South America; uncommon islands of Caribbean.

BLACK GRUNT   *Haemulon bonariense*
SIZE: 7-10 in., max. 12 in.   Grunts – Haemulidae
ID: Black scales join to form numerous thin oblique stripes on body. Silvery to pearly gray with dusky tail; large eye with gold tints around iris. Normally drift or swim in small schools, but occasionally solitary. **RANGE:** Common to occasional southern Caribbean; rare balance of Caribbean.

TOMTATE   *Haemulon aurolineatum*
SIZE: 5-8 in., max. 10 in.   Grunts – Haemulidae
ID: Prominent yellow to bronze stripe runs from snout through eye to base of tail; another thinner stripe on back. Silvery white to tan body. May have additional thin stripes on body. One of the smaller grunts. **RANGE:** Common to occasional Caribbean, Bahamas, S. Florida.

BOGA   *Haemulon vittata*
SIZE: 5-7 in., max. 9 in.   Grunts – Haemulidae
ID: Thin body stripes in yellow, blue and black on silvery blue cylindrical body. Snout often yellowish. Rear base of foredorsal fin connects with front base of second dorsal fin. **RANGE:** Common to occasional Caribbean, Bahamas, S. Florida.

LATIN GRUNT   *Haemulon steindachneri*
SIZE: 6-9 in., max. 11 in.   Grunts – Haemulidae
ID: Large black spot on base of tail. Silvery to pearly gray with dusky tail; dusky scales join to form numerous thin oblique stripes on body; large eye with gold tints around iris. **RANGE:** Common to occasional Southern Caribbean; not reported Bahamas, S. Florida or remainder of Caribbean.

STRIPED GRUNT   *Haemulon striatum*
SIZE: 6-9 in., max. 11 in.   Grunts – Haemulidae
ID: Normally have five yellow to brown stripes on upper body with no stripes on belly. Silver to white; head and back occasionally dusky; tail may be dark. Short snout; eyes near mouth. **RANGE:** Uncommon S. Florida; rare Caribbean, Bahamas.

COTTONWICK *Haemulon melanurum*
SIZE: 7-10 in., max. 13 in. Grunts – Haemulidae
ID: **Bold, black stripe on dorsal fin continues to form a "V" on tail.** Narrow, pale yellow horizontal stripes over white to silver background. Stripe begins on snout, runs across eye. RANGE: Occasional S. Florida; uncommon Caribbean, Bahamas.

SPANISH GRUNT *Haemulon macrostomum*
SIZE: 10-15 in., max. 17 in. Grunts – Haemulidae
ID: **Bold black stripes on upper body with yellow-green area between dorsal fin and first stripe.** Silver-gray with yellow pectoral fin and yellow borders on rear dorsal, anal and tail fins. Black stripe runs from eye to tail. **RANGE:** Common S. Florida; occasional to uncommon Caribbean, Bahamas.

MARGATE (WHITE) *Haemulon album*
SIZE: 1-1½ ft., max 2½ ft. Grunts – Haemulidae
ID: Largest of grunts. **High back profile and small eye with white iris.** Normally pearl gray and unmarked, but may have dusky spots over the body and three faint stripes at and above lateral line. Dorsal and tail fins are usually dusky. RANGE: Occasional Caribbean, Bahamas, S. Florida.

BLACK MARGATE *Anisotremus surinamensis*
SIZE: 1-1½ ft., max 2 ft. Grunts – Haemulidae
ID: **Dark patch behind pectoral fin.** Silvery-gray with high back profile. Scales on back have dark centers; fins dusky. Drift alone or in small groups near caves, ledge overhangs and other dark recesses. RANGE: Occasional Caribbean, Bahamas, S. Florida.

PORKFISH *Anisotremus virginicus*
SIZE: 6-10 in., max. 14 in. Grunts – Haemulidae
ID: **Two bold black diagonal bands on head.** Bright yellow-gold and silver with high back profile. Solitary or in small, loose groups. **RANGE:** Common S. Florida especially Keys; occasional to rare Caribbean; occasional Bahamas.

Porkfish – Juvenile SIZE: 2-3½ in.
ID: Yellow head, foredorsal and ventral fins with translucent to pearly white body; two black stripes and black spot on white tail.

Snappers

YELLOWTAIL SNAPPER *Ocyurus chrysurus*
SIZE: 1-2 ft., max. 2½ ft.   Snappers – Lutjanidae
ID: **Brilliant yellow midbody stripe and tail.** Silvery to white, often tinged with blue. May have yellow spots on upper body. Tail deeply forked. Swim alone or in loose schools or aggregations, usually well above bottom. **RANGE:** Abundant to common Caribbean, Bahamas, S. Florida.

GRAY SNAPPER *Lutjanus griseus*
SIZE: 10-18 in., max. 2 ft.   Snappers – Lutjanidae
ID: Vary from pale gray to dark gray or reddish brown; often tinged with olive, bronze or red; may lighten or darken dramatically. Often dark diagonal band through eye, especially in shallow habitats. Tail may have dark margin. **RANGE:** Common to occasional Caribbean, Bahamas, S. Florida.

CUBERA SNAPPER *Lutjanus cyanopterus*
SIZE: 1½-3 ft., max. 5 ft.   Snappers – Lutjanidae
ID: **Occasionally display bars of varying intensity on back.** Vary from silvery steel gray to dark brown, occasionally with purplish sheen; may lighten or darken dramatically. Solitary; largest snapper. **RANGE:** Occasional to uncommon Caribbean, Bahamas, S. Florida.

DOG SNAPPER *Lutjanus jocu*
SIZE: 1½-2½ ft., max. 3 ft.   Snappers – Lutjanidae
ID: **White to whitish triangular patch under eye, although occasionally pale, always visible.** Silvery to yellowish or copper brown; may lighten or darken dramatically. Two large, fanglike teeth at front of upper jaw. **RANGE:** Occasional to uncommon Caribbean, Bahamas, S. Florida.

MUTTON SNAPPER *Lutjanus analis*
SIZE: 1-2 ft., max. 2½ ft.   Snappers – Lutjanidae
ID: **Pale blue lines below eye.** Silver to gray, reddish brown or maroon; fins have reddish tint. Always display dark spot toward rear back. Adults develop a high back profile. **RANGE:** Occasional Caribbean, Bahamas, S. Florida.

Mutton Snapper – Phase
ID: May lighten or darken dramatically; occasionally display dark bars. Drift above bottom, most commonly over sand, but also reefs and seagrass beds.

SCHOOLMASTER *Lutjanus apodus*
SIZE: 10-18 in., max. 2 ft. Snappers – Lutjanidae
ID: Fins yellow. Silver to copper; often display faint darkish bars on back. Drift in small to medium size groups just above reefs and in shade of large coral structures, especially large gorgonians. **RANGE:** Abundant to common Caribbean; common Bahamas, S. Florida.

Schoolmaster – Juvenile **SIZE:** 1½ -3 in.
ID: Yellow body and fins with white bars on back and sides. Dark diagonal band runs through eye. Often inhabit shallow bays, inlets and mangrove lagoons.

MAHOGANY SNAPPER *Lutjanus mahogoni*
SIZE: 7-12 in., max. 15 in. Snappers – Lutjanidae
ID: Reddish margin on tail (may be quite narrow and pale) Silver to white, often with reddish tinge. Reddish border on dorsal and anal fins. Often have dark spot below rear dorsal fin. **RANGE:** Common to occasional Caribbean, Bahamas and S. Florida.

Mahogany Snapper – Young Adult **SIZE:** 1½ -3 in.
ID: White body and yellow to white fins with red margins on dorsal and tail fins. Inhabit shallow patch reefs. Juvenile Mahogany Snapper and Lane Snapper are nearly identical, and cannot be reliably differentiated underwater.

LANE SNAPPER *Lutjanus synagris*
SIZE: 8-12 in., max. 15 in. Snappers – Lutjanidae
ID: Several faint yellow to pink body stripes over silvery body. Pectoral, ventral and anal fins often yellow; dorsal and tail fins often reddish, also has uncommon pinkish phase. Black spot just below rear dorsal fin occasionally absent. **RANGE:** Common S. Florida; occasional Caribbean, Bahamas.

Lane Snapper – Juvenile **SIZE:** 1½ -6 in.
ID: Tail translucent occasionally with reddish margin. Inhabit shallow patch reefs, often in loose groups. Lane Snapper and Mahogany Snapper are nearly identical, and cannot be reliably differentiated underwater.

IDENTIFICATION GROUP 4

Damselfishes – Chromis/Damselfishes
Hamlets/Sea Basses

This ID Group consists of small fishes (generally three to six inches) that have a "perch-like" or oval profile.

Damselfishes
9 species, pg. 37

Chromis/Damselfishes
5 species, pg. 40

Hamlets/Sea Basses
10 species, pg. 42

Damselfishes, Pomacentridae – These energetic little fishes are an evident part of the coral reef community. The most distinctive (but difficult to observe) family characteristic is a single nostril on each side of the snout, rather than the usual two. Although most of the adults are drab, the juveniles are quite colorful. Cocoa, Dusky, Longfin and Threespot Damselfishes spend their days busily tending and patrolling a private algae patch that is pugnaciously defended from intruders. When the domains of these notorious nippers are threatened, the fishes dart back and forth with fins erect, ready to attack. Divers lingering nearby may receive a sharp nip on exposed skin. Egg clusters are also defended in a similar manner by guardian males. Bicolor Damselfish, one of the most common fish in the Caribbean, feed in the water column in small groups, plucking zooplankton from the currents. The feeding height is limited by size, with even the largest males rising no further than five feet above the protection of shelter holes. When predators or divers approach, the fish drop to the bottom and remain near cover until the threat passes. Distinguishing between the dark-bodied Longfin, Dusky, Beaugregory and Cocoa Damselfish is a bit difficult; however, slight differences make underwater identification possible. Except for the two sergeants in genus *Abudefduf*, juvenile damselfishes differ dramatically from adults; and, although the juveniles are similar in appearance, they are easily identified to species.

Chromis/Damselfishes, Pomacentridae – Damselfishes in genus *Chromis* are discussed separately because the group carries its own common name, and its members are somewhat different in appearance and behavior. The Blue and Brown Chromis are the most frequently seen species. Both are somewhat elongate plankton pickers with deeply forked tails. During the day Brown Chromis traditionally feed high above outer reef slopes in huge aggregations, while Blue Chromis form small groups that feed just above low profile reef structures.

Hamlets/Sea Basses, Serranidae – Hamlets, members of the sea bass family, are discussed in this ID Group because, in appearance and size, they closely resemble damselfish. Their relatives, groupers and basses, are discussed in the next ID Group—Heavy Bodies/Large Lips. The hamlets' flat head profile easily distinguishes them from damselfishes, which have rounded heads. Most are quite colorful, small (generally three to five inches), and have nearly identical body shapes; however, their distinctive color patterns and markings, generally make identification simple.

Within the scientific community, there has been a long-running debate whether hamlets are different species or simply a single species, *Hypoplectrus unicolor*, with different color and marking phases. Aquarium-based observations and experiments indicate individuals of like color patterns and markings usually mate together. On rare occasion, however, especially when a similar appearing mate is not present, different appearing individuals will mate producing offspring that do not easily fit into the dozen or so common color patterns and markings. These hybrid hamlets make up about three percent of the hamlet population.

LONGFIN DAMSELFISH *Stegastes diencaeus*
SIZE: 2-4 in., max. 6 in. Damselfishes – Pomacentridae
ID: Thin bright blue edge on anal fin. Dorsal and anal fins extend beyond base of tail. (Similar Dusky Damselfish [next] dorsal and anal fins are shorter and do not extend beyond tail base.) Brownish gray to nearly black. **RANGE:** Common Caribbean, Bahamas, S. Florida.

Longfin Damselfish – Juvenile **SIZE:** 1-3 in
ID: Yellow-gold with brilliant blue lines from snout to back usually over dusky undercolor (never display the blue undercolor of Cocoa Damselfish [pg. 38]) and Beaugregory [pg. 39]).

DUSKY DAMSELFISH *Stegastes adustus*
SIZE: 2-4 in., max. 5 in. Damselfishes – Pomacentridae
ID: Narrow dark edge on anal fin. Dorsal and anal fins extend only to insertion of tail fin rays into tail base. Vary from light brown to dark chocolate brown. Although their depth ranges overlap, tend to live more shallow than Longfin Damselfish [above]. **RANGE:** Occasional Caribbean, Bahamas, S. Florida.

Dusky Damselfish – Juvenile **SIZE:** 1-2 in.
ID: Bluish silver-gray with **orange wash from snout across nape continuing to near end of spinous dorsal fin.** Blue dot/dash markings on head and back. Large dark spot on dorsal fin and small dark spot on tail base, both ringed in white to electric blue. Inhabit shallows, often in surge. Quite wary.

THREESPOT DAMSELFISH *Stegastes planifrons*
SIZE: 3-4 in., max. 5 in. Damselfishes – Pomacentridae
ID: Yellow-gold crescent above eyes. Dark spot on base of pectoral fin, and black saddle on upper base of tail. Vary from yellowish brown to tan and gray; become darker with age. Head profile of nape and snout is straight. **RANGE:** Abundant to common Caribbean; common Bahamas, S. Florida.

Threespot Damselfish – Juvenile **SIZE:** 1-2 in.
ID: Bright yellow with black saddle on upper base of tail, which is retained into adulthood. Larger second dot on back and dorsal fin is lost with maturity.

COCOA DAMSELFISH   *Stegastes xanthurus*
SIZE: 3-4 in., max. 5 in.   Damselfishes – Pomacentridae
ID: Dark diagonal lines on scale row edges extend down sides. Juveniles have dark spot on mid-dorsal fin that extends onto body, this spots occasionally persists into adulthood.
RANGE: Common to occasional Caribbean, Bahamas and S. Florida.

Cocoa Damselfish – Variation
ID: Typically Cocoa Damselfish display a dark spot on the base of the tail, but occasionally this spot is absent as pictured above. Adults are variable shades of brown occasionally with yellow or yellowish undersides. Note smoothly pointed snout which contrasts with blunt somewhat concave snout of similar appearing Beaugregory [facing page].

Cocoa Damselfish – Sub-adult   **SIZE:** 2-3 in.
ID: Sub-adults and juveniles occasionally have blue spots on body scales which disappear as they mature. This may cause confusion with Beaugregories where blue spots persist through adulthood. The dark diagonal lines on scale row edges always distinguish the Cocoa Damselfish.

Cocoa Damselfish – Juvenile   **SIZE:** 1-2 in.
ID: Large dark spot on dorsal fin, ringed in bright blue, extends slightly onto body. Yellow body with greenish tint. Dark diagonal lines extend down body; usually a light blue and black spot on tail base.

BICOLOR DAMSELFISH   *Stegastes partitus*
SIZE: 2-3½ in., max. 4 in.   Damselfishes – Pomacentridae
ID: Forebody usually black. Boundary between dark and pale areas is highly variable; dark area may cover only upper head or extend past midbody to base of tail. **RANGE:** Abundant to common Caribbean, Bahamas, S. Florida.

Bicolor Damselfish – Variation
ID: Pale area often yellowish near boundary, especially toward belly. Pale fins may have bluish cast. A few individuals are completely light or dark. On rare occasions, there is a reverse color phase. Inhabit patch reefs and low-profile reef tops living in colonies often numbering a dozen or more. Egg-guarding males aggressively defend territories.

BEAUGREGORY *Stegastes leucostictus*

SIZE: 2-3 in., max. 4 in.   Damselfishes – Pomacentridae

ID: A scattering of small blue dots centered on many body scales. When compared to Cocoa Damselfish [previous page] only faint diagonal lines on scale row edges extend down body. **RANGE:** Common to occasional Caribbean, Bahamas and S. Florida.

Beaugregory – Young Adult   **SIZE:** 2-3 in.

ID: Blunt somewhat concave snout. Black spot on dorsal fin does not extend onto body. Variable shades of brown, middle aged and young adults often have yellow tail, ventral and anal fins.

Beaugregory – Sub-Adult   **SIZE:** 1^1/$_2$-2^1/$_2$ in.

ID: On rare occasions Beaugregory may display a dark spot on base of tail, which can cause confusion with the more common tail base spot on the Cocoa Damselfish. However, the black spot, completely contained within the dorsal fin, confirms identification as a Beaugregory.

Beaugregory – Juvenile   **SIZE:** 1-2 in.

ID: Large dark spot on dorsal fin, ringed in bright blue, does not extend onto body. Yellow body with no dark diagonal scale rows.

SERGEANT MAJOR *Abudefduf saxatilis*

SIZE: 4-6 in., max. 7 in.   Damselfishes – Pomacentridae

ID: Five black body bars. Upper body usually yellowish, occasionally with shades of green to blue, with white to bluish silver or light gray below. Males become dark blue when reproductively active. Numerous habitats. **RANGE:** Abundant to common Caribbean, Bahamas, S. Florida.

NIGHT SERGEANT *Abudefduf taurus*

SIZE: 5-8 in., max. 10 in.   Damselfishes – Pomacentridae

ID: Five dark brown body bars. Hues of brown; may have a blue-green tint. Upper lip slightly overhangs lower. Inhabit shallow, rocky inshore surge zones. **RANGE:** Occasional Caribbean, Bahamas, S. Florida.

YELLOWTAIL DAMSELFISH
Microspathodon chrysurus
Damselfishes – Pomacentridae
SIZE: 4-6$\frac{1}{2}$ in., max. 7$\frac{1}{2}$ in.
ID: Yellow tail. Dark body varies from brown to bluish black. Bright blue speckles on head, back and dorsal fin. Inhabit reef tops and stands of antler and fire corals. Maintain a small territory, but do not aggressively defend their domains. **RANGE:** Common to occasional Caribbean, Bahamas, S. Florida.

Yellowtail Damselfish – Phase
ID: Adults can quickly and temporarily change to a nearly solid gold color.

Yellowtail Damselfish – Juvenile   **SIZE:** 1$\frac{1}{2}$ -3 in.
ID: Brilliant blue dots on dark blue. (Juveniles occasionally referred to as "Jewelfish" because of these gemlike dots.) Inhabit shallows often in stands of fire coral. Translucent to whitish tail changes to yellow with maturity.

BROWN CHROMIS
Chromis multilineata
Chromis/Damselfishes – Pomacentridae
SIZE: 3-5$\frac{1}{2}$ in., max. 6$\frac{1}{2}$ in.
ID: Vary from brownish gray to olive-brown. Usually a white or pale yellow spot located just below last dorsal fin ray. May have black borders on tail (primarily in southern Caribbean). Slender, with deeply forked tail. Border of dorsal fin and tips of tail fin yellow and dark spot around base of pectoral fin. Feed on plankton in small to huge aggregations well above outer reef banks. **RANGE:** Abundant to common Caribbean, Bahamas, S. Florida.

BLUE CHROMIS
Chromis cyanea

SIZE: 3-4 in., max. 5 in. Chromis/Damselfishes
Pomacentridae

ID: Blue to purple with dark wash along back. Deeply forked tail with dark borders. Feed on plankton in small, loose aggregations just above low-profile or patch reefs. **RANGE:** Abundant Caribbean, Bahamas; common S. Florida.

YELLOWTAIL REEFFISH
Chromis enchrysura

SIZE: 2-3 in., max. 4 in. Chromis/Damselfishes – Pomacentridae

ID: Yellow to clear tail. **Bright, iridescent blue "V" on snout continues across upper eyes.** Blue upper body; blue or white underside; rear of dorsal and anal fins yellow to clear. Tend to form small clusters along deep dropoffs. **RANGE:** Occasional S. Florida; uncommon to rare Caribbean, Bahamas.

PURPLE REEFFISH
Chromis scotti

SIZE: 2-3 in., max. 4 in. Chromis/Damselfishes – Pomacentridae

ID: Bright blue crescent above upper part of eyes (disappears with age). Slate blue to navy blue; often with bright blue markings on head and back. Inhabit reefs below 80 ft. **RANGE:** Occasional S. Florida; uncommon to rare Caribbean, Bahamas.

Purple Reeffish – Juvenile
SIZE: 1-3 in.

ID: Brilliant blue with bright blue crescent above eye more apparent on juveniles than adults.

SUNSHINEFISH
Chromis insolata

SIZE: 2-3 in., max. 4 in. Chromis/Damselfishes – Pomacentridae

ID: Yellow or transparent rear soft dorsal fin and margin on tail. Green to olive, brown and dark brown upper body; belly may be pale to silvery gray; anal and pectoral fins often clear. Often have blue line that runs from snout across upper eye. **RANGE:** Common to occasional Caribbean, Bahamas, S. Florida.

Sunshinefish – Juvenile
SIZE: 1-2 in.

ID: Brilliant yellow to chartreuse upper body; brilliant blue to purple, lavender or dull olive below. Inhabit deep reefs and walls. Tend to cluster in small groups close to recesses near bottom, remaining around a single small coral head. Adults and juveniles often mix. Become more abundant with depth.

BARRED HAMLET
Hypoplectrus puella
Hamlets/Sea Basses – Serranidae
SIZE: 3½-4½ in., max. 6 in.
ID: Broad bar on midbody. Brown body bars over pale white to yellowish background. Bright blue vertical lines on head and around eyes, and spots on snout. Remain near bottom within limited feeding territories on or near reefs. Like most hamlet species usually inhabit depths between 20-50 ft.
RANGE: Most common hamlet in Caribbean, Bahamas; occasional S. Florida.

INDIGO HAMLET   *Hypoplectrus indigo*
SIZE: 3-4½ in., max. 5½ in. Hamlets/Sea Basses – Serranidae
ID: Blue and white bars. Wide medium blue to indigo bars separated by narrower white bars. Blue ventral fins; pectoral fins white or clear. **RANGE:** Common Cayman Islands, Jamaica and Bay Islands; occasional Belize and Bahamas; rare balance of Caribbean and S. Florida.

BUTTER HAMLET   *Hypoplectrus unicolor*
SIZE: 3-4½ in., max. 5 in.   Hamlets/Seabasses – Serranidae
ID: Large black saddle blotch on base of tail. Grayish white to yellow. Blue markings on head and gill cover; often have black spot on snout outlined in blue. Can pale or darken. **RANGE:** Most common hamlet in Florida Keys; occasional Caribbean, Bahamas.

YELLOWBELLY HAMLET   *Hypoplectrus aberrans*
SIZE: 3-4½ in., max. 5 in.   Hamlets/Sea Basses – Serranidae
ID: Yellow underside extends to tail. Dark brown to slate blue upper body. Dorsal fin yellowish brown lightening toward rear; other fins yellow. Head may have bluish cast and blue markings. **RANGE:** Uncommon Turks and Caicos, Caribbean; rare S. Florida; not reported Bahamas.

SHY HAMLET   *Hypoplectrus guttavarius*
SIZE: 3-4½ in., max. 5 in.   Hamlets/Sea Basses – Serranidae
ID: All fins are bright yellow. Yellow to gold, with dark area under dorsal fin that extends to cover entire base of tail. Bright blue markings on snout and head. **RANGE:** Occasional to uncommon Caribbean, Bahamas; rare S. Florida.

GOLDEN HAMLET   *Hypoplectrus gummigutta*
SIZE: 3-4¹/₂ in., max. 5 in.   Hamlets/Sea Basses – Serranidae
ID: Gold to yellow. Iridescent blue and black markings on face. **RANGE:** Occasional eastern and northwest Caribbean including Cuba; rare Bahamas, S. Florida and central Caribbean. Not reported southern Caribbean.

MASKED HAMLET   *Hypoplectrus providencianus*
SIZE: 3-4¹/₂ in., max. 5 in.   Hamlets/Sea Basses – Serranidae
ID: Black mask extends triangularly down from eyes. Pale with bluish or brownish cast. Ventral fins dark with bluish cast; black borders on tail and upper pectoral fin. **RANGE:** Uncommon Cayman Is., Belize, Honduras and Providencia Is. Not reported balance of Caribbean, Bahamas, S. Florida.

BLACK HAMLET   *Hypoplectrus nigricans*
SIZE: 3-4¹/₂ in., max. 6 in.   Hamlets/Sea Basses – Serranidae
ID: Solid dark color. Entire body dark bluish brown to black. Ventral fins unusually long. **RANGE:** Occasional Caribbean; uncommon Bahamas, S. Florida.

YELLOWTAIL HAMLET   *Hypoplectrus chlorurus*
SIZE: 3-4¹/₂ in., max. 5 in.   Hamlets/Sea Basses – Serranidae
ID: Yellow tail. Body and fins vary from dark brown to dark blue, navy blue and black. **RANGE:** Common to occasional southern and southeastern Caribbean; rare western Caribbean and Bahamas; not reported S. Florida.

BLUE HAMLET   *Hypoplectrus gemma*
SIZE: 3-4¹/₂ in., max. 5 in.   Hamlets/Sea Basses – Serranidae
ID: Bright iridescent blue with thin, dark borders on tail. RANGE: Common to occasional S. Florida and Keys. Not reported Bahamas or Caribbean.

Hamlet – Juvenile   **SIZE:** 1¹/₂-2 in.
ID: Prominent black and white markings on tail base are typical of all juvenile hamlets. Body tan to occasionally golden. With maturity acquire adult color and markings.

Heavy Bodies/Large Lips
Groupers/Sea Basses – Basses/Sea Basses
Soapfishes/Sea Basses – Basslets

This ID Group consists of fishes with strong, well-built, "basslike" bodies. They have large mouths and lips, and a jutting lower jaw. The long, continuous dorsal fin is noticeably divided into two parts. The fore portion is constructed of sharp spines that can be held erect or lowered; the rear is soft and quite flexible.

Groupers/Sea Basses	Basses/Sea Basses	Soapfishes/Sea Basses	Basslets
15 species, pg. 45	19 species, pg. 50	3 species, pg. 54	4 species, pg. 55

Groupers, Epinephelidae – Groupers are the best known members of the sea bass family. All have strong, stout bodies and large mouths. They vary in size from the giant Goliath Grouper that grows to seven feet to the one-foot Graysby. They are solitary carnivores that live near the bottom. Most of their days are spent lurking in the shadows of reefs, ledges and wrecks where larger species blend with the background.

Although awkward in appearance, these fishes can cover short distances quickly. Fishes or crustaceans are drawn into their gullets by the powerful suction created when they open their large mouths. Held securely by thousands of small, rasplike teeth that cover the jaws, tongue and palate, the prey is swallowed whole. Groupers are hermaphroditic, beginning life as females and later changing into males with maturity. Many of the larger groupers, such as Yellowfin Grouper and Yellowmouth Grouper are difficult to distinguish because of their ability to radically change both colors and markings.

Basses/Sea Basses, Serranidae – Often called basses, these members of the sea bass family are generally more colorful than groupers. Most are small, two to four inches, whereas a few grow to nearly a foot. All are stocky like groupers, but tend to be more cylindrical and elongate. Basses are fundamentally bottom-oriented crustacean feeders, except the Atlantic Creolefish, which pluck zooplankton from open water high above the reef. Generally, the basses' distinctive color and markings make them easy to identify to species. Note: Hamlets of the genus *Hypoplectrus* are also members of the sea bass family, but because of their small, oval shape, they are discussed in the previous ID Group—Small Ovals.

Soapfishes/Sea Basses, Serranidae – Soapfishes were formerly classified as a separate family, Grammistidae, but are now a subfamily of the sea bass family. Their bodies are covered with mucus that produces soaplike bubbles when they are caught and handled. Typically soapfishes have elongate, pointed heads with upturned mouths, protruding lower jaws, and rounded tail fins. Most grow to less than one foot. They generally inhabit shallower waters, are solitary, reclusive night-feeders that tend to lie on the bottom and often lean against the back of a protective overhang during the day.

Basslets, Grammatidae – This family of small fishes, one to four inches, is closely related to the sea bass, but lacks a continuous lateral line. These solitary, secretive fishes generally inhabit undercuts and crevices on deeper reefs and walls, although the common Fairy Basslet often inhabit shallower depths.

GOLIATH GROUPER
Epinephelus itajara
Groupers – Epinephelidae
SIZE: 4-6 ft., max. 8 ft.
ID: Largest fish observed on the reefs. **Small dark spots over body and fins.** Yellowish brown to olive-green. Can pale or darken. Tail fin rounded. Inhabit reefs with deep crevices, ledge overhangs and caves, also wrecks. **RANGE:** Occasional S. Florida; uncommon Caribbean, Bahamas.

NASSAU GROUPER   *Epinephelus striatus*
SIZE: 1-2 ft., max. 4 ft.   Groupers – Epinephelidae
ID: Black saddle spot on base of tail. Five irregular, olive-brown bars over light background. Diagonal bar from snout across eye to start of dorsal fin. Can change from pale to almost black. Foreorsal fin notched between spines. **RANGE:** Occasional Bahamas; uncommon Caribbean, S. Florida.

RED GROUPER   *Epinephelus morio*
SIZE: 1-2 ft., max. 3 ft.   Groupers – Epinephelidae
ID: Foredorsal fin has smooth, straight edge (not notched). Variable earthtones, usually reddish brown with small, scattered whitish blotches. May display bars and blotches. Can change color, pale or darken. **RANGE:** Occasional S. Florida; rare Caribbean, Bahamas.

MISTY GROUPER   *Hyporthodus mystacinus*
SIZE: 3-6 in. (adults to 5 ft.)   Groupers – Epinephelidae
ID: JUVENILE – Eight to nine black and white bars and dark band on base of tail. White to dark brown. Juveniles occasionally inhabit mid-range to deep reefs. Adults inhabit waters well below safe diving limits. **RANGE:** Rare Caribbean, Bahamas, S. Florida.

SNOWY GROUPER   *Hyporthodus niveatus*
SIZE: 2-8 in. (adults to 3 ft.)   Groupers – Epinephelidae
ID: JUVENILE – Large, black circular saddle over base of tail and rows of bold white spots on body. Dark brown to orangish brown; tail pale to yellow. Juveniles occasionally inhabit deep reefs. Adults live well below safe diving limits. **RANGE:** Rare Caribbean, Bahamas, S. Florida.

Groupers/Sea Basses

MARBLED GROUPER   *Dermatolepis inermis*
SIZE: 1-2 ft., max. 3 ft.   Groupers – Epinephelidae
ID: JUVENILE – Dark brown to black with large white blotches. Steep, straight head profile. Juveniles occasionally inhabit deep reefs. Adults commonly live well below safe diving limits. **RANGE:** Rare Caribbean, Bahamas, S. Florida.

RED HIND   *Epinephelus guttatus*
SIZE: 10-15 in., max. 2 ft.   Groupers – Epinephelidae
ID: Tail and rear fins have black margin edged in white. Reddish spots over whitish background (no spots on tail or dorsal fin). **RANGE:** Common to occasional Caribbean; Bahamas; uncommon S. Florida.

ROCK HIND   *Epinephelus adscensionis*
SIZE: 8-14 in., max. 2 ft.   Groupers – Epinephelidae
ID: Black saddle blotch on base of tail. Reddish to dark dots cover body and all fins. One to four pale or dark blotches along back, below dorsal fin. Can pale to almost white or darken dramatically. **RANGE:** Occasional to uncommon Caribbean, Bahamas, S. Florida.

Rock Hind – Juvenile   **SIZE:** 3-10 in.
ID: Greenish brown with numerous black and white spots and yellow highlights on fins.

GRAYSBY   *Cephalopholis cruentata*
SIZE: 6-10 in., max. 1 ft.   Groupers – Epinephelidae
ID: Three to five pale or dark spots along base of dorsal fin. Light reddish brown to gray, with darker orangish brown spots over body. Can change color, pale or darken. Tail more rounded than similar species. **RANGE:** Abundant Caribbean; common Bahamas, S. Florida.

Graysby – Juvenile   **SIZE:** 1-5 in.
ID: White band runs from nape, between eyes to lower lip. Tan to brown with vague spotting. Often display yellow wash on back and dorsal fins.

CONEY
Cephalopholis fulva
Groupers – Epinephelidae
SIZE: 6-10 in., max. 16 in.

ID: Two black dots on lower lip; two black dots behind dorsal fin on base of tail. Body covered with small blue to pale or dark dots. Identification by color impractical because of several color variations. Shades of reddish brown to brown most common; also has a bicolor variation (upper dark and lower pale); and an uncommon brilliant golden variation. **RANGE:** Common Caribbean, Bahamas; occasional S. Florida.

Coney – Bicolor Variation
ID: Brown to reddish upper body with white below; body covered with sprinkling of dark dots. White tail.

Coney – Golden Variation
ID: Solid yellow with scattering of dark spots; some blue outlining on fins. Distinguished, like other variations, by two dark spots on lower lip and **two dark spots on base of tail**.

Coney – Juvenile   **SIZE:** 1-5 in.
ID: Most common juvenile color and marking variation with reddish brown upper body and pale below, covered with dark spotting. **Four spots on lower lip** and two dark spots on base of tail.

Coney – Juvenile   **SIZE:** 1-5 in.
ID: Yellow with scattering of blue and black spots. Four spots on lower lip and two dark spots on base of tail.

Groupers/Sea Basses

TIGER GROUPER
Mycteroperca tigris
Groupers – Epinephelidae
SIZE: 1-2 ft., max. 3½ ft.
ID: Dramatic "tiger-stripe" bars. Often heavily covered with spotting and blotches. Can dramatically change color of markings from tan to red or black, also pale or darken. Occasionally bright red, especially in cleaning stations. **RANGE:** Common to occasional NW Caribbean, Bahamas; uncommon to rare central and eastern Caribbean, S. Florida.

Tiger Grouper – Tan phase
ID: Common tan phase.

Tiger Grouper – Black phase
ID: Rare black phase.

Tiger Grouper – Juvenile   **SIZE:** 2-4 in.
ID: Yellow with **dusky midbody stripe.**

GAG   *Mycteroperca microlepis*
SIZE: 1½ - 2 ft., max. 3 ft.   Groupers – Epinephelidae
ID: Dark lines radiate from eye. Pale to dark gray, dusky scrawled or blotch markings on body, dusky tail with thin blue margin. **RANGE:** Common Gulf of Mexico; occasional South to northeast Florida; absent Bahamas and Caribbean.

YELLOWMOUTH GROUPER   *Mycteroperca interstitialis*

SIZE: 1-2 ft., max. 2½ ft.

Groupers – Epinephelidae

ID: Distinct yellow around corners of mouth. Brown to brownish gray; color may be uniform or display pattern of close-set dots and occasionally blotches. Can pale or darken dramatically. **RANGE:** Uncommon Caribbean, Bahamas, S. Florida.

Yellowmouth Grouper – Phase

ID: Blotched phase.

Yellowmouth Grouper – Juvenile   **SIZE:** 3½ -10 in.

ID: Dark upper and white lower body with dark margins on tail and yellow wash on dorsal fin that may extend to back.

YELLOWFIN GROUPER   *Mycteroperca venenosa*

SIZE: 1-2 ft., max. 3 ft.

Groupers – Epinephelidae

ID: Outer third of pectoral fin is pale to bright yellow. Rounded blotches over light background can be black, gray, brown, olive-green or red [pictured below]. Can dramatically change color, pale or darken. **RANGE:** Occasional Caribbean, Bahamas, S. Florida.

Yellowfin Grouper – Phase

ID: Common phase with black, rounded blotches and reddish highlights.

Yellowfin Grouper – Phase

ID: Pale background with rounded red blotches.

BLACK GROUPER
Mycteroperca bonaci
Groupers – Epinephelidae
SIZE: 1½-3 ft., max. 4 ft.
ID: Thin, pale to yellow margin on pectoral fins. Vary from reddish brown to black. Can pale or darken until markings become indistinct. Ends of the large rectangular blotches on upper body are nearly square. Tail has wide, black margin with thin, white edge. Often display yellow wash around corners of mouth.
RANGE: Occasional S. Florida, Bahamas, northwestern Caribbean; uncommon to rare central and eastern Caribbean.

Black Grouper – Phase
ID: Body can lighten clearly displaying dark borders on fins with thin edging.

Black Grouper – Phase
ID: Distinctly displaying square blotches on upper body.

WESTERN COMB GROUPER   *Mycteroperca acutirostris*
SIZE: 1-2 ft., max. 2½ ft.   Groupers – Epinephelidae
ID: Three to four dark lines extend from eye and cheek to just beyond gill cover. Brownish to gray. Small whitish blotches over upper body and fins. Markings become less distinct with age. **RANGE:** Occasional southern Caribbean; rare or absent northern Caribbean, Bahamas, S. Florida.

SCAMP   *Mycteroperca phenax*
SIZE: 1-1½ in., max. 2 ft.   Groupers – Epinephelidae
ID: Dusky tail with pale margin. Light brown to gray, dark rectangular blotches (paw prints) form vague horizontal stripes on body. **RANGE:** Occasional to rare Florida and continental coast to northern South America; absent Caribbean, Islands.

DWARF SAND PERCH · *Diplectrum bivittatum*

SIZE: 4-6 in., max 10 in. Basses/Sea Basses – Serranidae

ID: Tan with dark mid-body stripe from snout to tail and two additional stripes on back; several blue lines on lower head; occasionally display 5-6 wide dark bars on back. **RANGE:** Occasional Caribbean Antilles and coasts of Central and South America; rare S. Florida.

HARLEQUIN BASS
Serranus tigrinus

Basses/Sea Basses – Serranidae

SIZE: 2¹/₂-3¹/₂ in., max. 4 in.

ID: Dark "tiger-stripe" bars. Whitish upper body undercolor; lower body pale yellow. Series of dark dots form diffuse horizontal lines on body. Head more pointed than other family members. Often seen in mated pairs hunting together within small territories adjacent to reefs. Easily approached. **RANGE:** Common Caribbean, Bahamas, S. Florida.

SAND PERCH · *Diplectrum formosum*

SIZE: 5-9 in., max. 1 ft. Basses/Sea Basses – Serranidae

ID: Pale blue line markings on head. Thin, blue body stripes with tan wash between on upper body; dark bars tend to be more distinct when at rest, stripes more apparent when moving. **RANGE:** Occasional S. Florida; uncommon southern Caribbean; rare or absent remainder of Caribbean, Bahamas.

TWINSPOT BASS · *Serranus flaviventris*

SIZE: 1¹/₂-2¹/₂ in., max. 3 in. Basses/Sea Basses – Serranidae

ID: Pair of dark spots on base of tail. Brown with dark spots and occasionally pale bars; dark streak from snout through eye and onto body; yellow area around base of ventral fin. Inhabit shallow, turbid water with rubble and seagrass. **RANGE:** Uncommon Caribbean; not reported Bahamas, S. Florida.

SNOW BASS · *Serranus chionaraia*

SIZE: 1¹/₄-1³/₄ in., max. 2 in. Basses/Sea Basses – Serranidae

ID: White belly and series of dark spots along upper and lower borders of tail. White undercolor with several stripe markings on head and bar markings in shades of brown on upper and rear body. **RANGE:** Uncommon southern and western Caribbean, S. Florida.

Basses/Sea Basses

SADDLE BASS *Serranus notospilus*
SIZE: 2-3 in., max. 4 in.   Basses/Sea Basses – Serranidae
ID: Whitish rectangular patch with bright, white leading edge on midbelly. Reddish undercolor; brown bands extend from back to belly.; reddish brown band below eye and reddish margin on tail. Typically deepwater species but shallow Venezuela. **RANGE:** Rare Puerto Rico to southern Caribbean.

TATTLER BASS *Serranus phoebe*
SIZE: 2 1/2-5 in., max. 6 in.   Basses/Sea Basses – Serranidae
ID: Dark bar from foredorsal fin to belly. White undercolor. Occasionally have a few additional minor brownish bars and stripes. Dark midbody stripe from behind white patch to tail. Inhabit deep sand areas below 85 ft. **RANGE:** Uncommon to rare Caribbean, S. Florida; not reported Bahamas.

LANTERN BASS *Serranus baldwini*
SIZE: 1 1/2-2 in., max. 2 1/2 in.   Basses/Sea Basses – Serranidae
ID: Obvious row of dark, rectangular blotches on lower side. Body marked with rows of dark to orange rectangular blotches and spots over white. Band of four black spots on base of tail. Frequently inhabit sandy rubble. **RANGE:** Occasional Caribbean, S. Florida; uncommon Bahamas.

CHALK BASS *Serranus tortugarum*
SIZE: 1 1/2-3 in., max. 3 1/2 in.   Basses/Sea Basses – Serranidae
ID: Series of pale and dark bars across back. Usually bluish, but can be orange to brown. Hover in small groups over sand bottoms and coral rubble below 35 ft. **RANGE:** Occasional Caribbean, Bahamas, S. Florida.

TOBACCOFISH *Serranus tabacarius*
SIZE: 3-4 1/2 in., max. 7 in.   Basses/Sea Basses – Serranidae
ID: Midbody shades of orange to brown (tobacco color). Alternating series of dark and white to yellow or salmon blotches along back. Hover just above bottom; usually below 30 ft. **RANGE:** Common Caribbean; occasional Bahamas, S. Florida.

ORANGEBACK BASS *Serranus annularis*
SIZE: 1 1/2 -2 in., max. 2 1/2 in.   Basses/Sea Basses – Serranidae
ID: Two orange to yellow squares outlined in black behind eyes. Orange markings on head; dark orangish brown pattern of markings on back; orange to yellow rectangular markings on the white undercolor of midbody and belly. **RANGE:** Uncommon to rare Caribbean, Bahamas, S. Florida.

PEPPERMINT BASSLET
Liopropoma rubre
Basses/Sea Basses – Serranidae
SIZE: 1½-3 in., max. 3½ in.
ID: Dark spot on rear dorsal and on anal fin. Boldly marked with maroon, pinkish rose and yellowish gold stripes. Two blotches on tail are joined. (Compare similar Candy Basslet [next] distinguished by lack of spot on anal fin and dark blotches on tail that do not join.) Reclusive; inhabit dark recesses, ledges and plate corals. Wary, but somewhat curious; usually slowly retreat deep into recesses when first approached, but typically reappear in openings once or twice. Best viewed with a light.
RANGE: Common to occasional Caribbean, Bahamas, S. Florida.

CANDY BASSLET
Liopropoma carmabi
SIZE: 1-1¾ in., max. 2 in.   Basses/Sea Basses – Serranidae
ID: Lacks dark spot on anal fin. Boldly marked with stripes in shades of light brown to red-brown or yellow-brown alternating with red to maroon; stripes may be occasionally yellow to lavender or blue. Wary; inhabit dark recesses below 50 ft. **RANGE:** Uncommon Caribbean, Bahamas, S. Florida.

CAVE BASSLET
Liopropoma mowbrayi
SIZE: 1½-3 in., max. 3½ in.   Basses/Sea Basses – Serranidae
ID: Black submarginal band on tail. Salmon to dark red. Yellow stripe runs from tip of snout to eye. Margin of second dorsal fin and tail white to brilliant blue. Below 80 ft.
RANGE: Occasional southern, central and western Caribbean; uncommon Bahamas, northern Caribbean; rare S. Florida.

SCHOOL BASS
Schultzea beta
SIZE: 1-2 in., max. 4 in.   Basses/Sea Basses – Serranidae
ID: Yellow tail; white body with three reddish brown stripes; dark stripe from snout through eye. In small groups, usually below 50 feet on wall and steep dropoffs. **RANGE:** Occasional Caribbean, Bahamas, S. Florida.

BANTAM BASS
Parasphyraenops incisus
SIZE: 1-1½ in., max. 1¾ in.   Basses/Sea Basses – Serranidae
ID: Dark spot on upper foredorsal fin. White with three wide reddish brown stripes. Gather in mixed aggregations with other small fishes along slopes below 30 ft. **RANGE:** Uncommon Jamaica, Puerto Rico and Virgin Islands to islands off South America.

Basses/Sea Basses – Soapfishes/Sea Basses – Basslets

ATLANTIC CREOLEFISH
Paranthias furcifer

Basses/Sea Basses – Serranidae

SIZE: 4-8 in., max. 10½ in.

ID: Bright red spot at base of pectoral fin. Vary from olive to bright reddish brown, often with a purplish cast; belly pale salmon. Three light or dark spots along back. Forked tail. Prefer deep reefs. Feed on plankton in small groups to large schools high in water column, but may hover near or just inside reef structure.
RANGE: Common central and southern Caribbean; uncommon Bahamas; rare northern Caribbean, S. Florida.

MUTTON HAMLET   *Alphestes afer*
SIZE: 5-10 in., max. 1 ft.   Basses/Sea Basses – Serranidae
ID: Eyes set close to tip of snout; red iris; pupil dark, often green. Mottled, blotched and occasionally banded in varying shades of reddish brown to orange-brown, olive and white.
RANGE: Uncommon Caribbean, Bahamas, S. Florida.

FRECKLED SOAPFISH   *Rypticus bistrispinus*
SIZE: 3-5 in., max. 6 in.   Soapfishes/Sea Basses – Serranidae
ID: Brown frecklelike spots cover body. Dark upper body with brown undercolor and closely set freckles commonly gradates to whitish belly with more widely spaced freckles. **RANGE:** Uncommon Caribbean, Bahamas, S. Florida.

GREATER SOAPFISH
Rypticus saponaceus

Soapfishes/Sea Basses – Serranidae

SIZE: 5-9 in., max. 13 in.

ID: Vary from drab reddish brown to gray; may have green or blue cast. Mottled and covered with pale indistinct blotches and spots. Solitary and inactive; often rest on bottom or lean against ledges or coral heads. Feed at night on small fishes, especially cardinalfishes. Their common name derives from the soaplike toxic mucus they secrete.
RANGE: Common to occasional Caribbean; uncommon Bahamas, S. Florida.

SPOTTED SOAPFISH *Rypticus subbifrenatus*

SIZE: 4-6 in., max. 7 in. Soapfishes/Sea Basses – Serranidae

ID: Random black spots with pale borders on body. Olive to brown; pale stripe often runs from lips across snout and nape, fading to dorsal fin; may have occasional random white spots. Pointed head with upturned mouth. **RANGE:** Uncommon Caribbean, Bahamas, S. Florida.

FAIRY BASSLET
Gramma loreto
Basslets – Grammatidae

SIZE: 1¹/₂-2¹/₂ in., max. 3 in.

ID: Bicolored — purple to violet front and yellow to gold rear with dark spot on dorsal fin. Several streaks on head run across eye. Flit about, in or near recesses. May orient bellies to ceilings of caves or ledges swimming upside-down. Inhabit moderate depths. **RANGE:** Common Caribbean, Bahamas; rare S. Florida.

THREELINE BASSLET *Lipogramma trilineatum*

SIZE: ³/₄ -1¹/₄ in., max. 1¹/₂ in. Basslets – Grammatidae

ID: Three, bluish to brilliant iridescent blue lines edged in black on head. Inhabit caves, recesses and deep cut ledge overhangs on deep reefs and walls where they often orient their belly to the ceiling swimming upside-down. **RANGE:** Occasional Caribbean, Bahamas, S. Florida.

BLACKCAP BASSLET *Gramma melacara*

SIZE: 2-3 in., max. 4 in. Basslets – Grammatidae

ID: "Black cap" from lip to foredorsal fin. Magenta to indigo. Faint gold lines on head, dots on body. Inhabit recesses in walls below 60 ft. **RANGE:** Common northwest and southern Caribbean; uncommon balance of Caribbean; not reported S. Florida and eastern Caribbean islands.

YELLOWCHEEK BASSLET *Gramma linki*

SIZE: 2-3 in., max. 4 in. Basslets – Grammatidae

ID: Yellow streaks run from below eye across gill cover. Vary from olive-green to blue, greenish blue most common. Can have faint gold dots on body. Inhabit recesses in walls below 60 ft. **RANGE:** Uncommon Caribbean, Bahamas; not reported S. Florida.

55

Swim with Pectoral Fins/Obvious Scales
Parrotfishes – Wrasses – Hogfishes/Wrasses
Razorfishes/Wrasses

This ID Group consists of fishes that primarily use their pectoral fins to swim. (A few other fishes also use their pectoral fins, but not as conspicuously.) They also have even rows of large, noticeable scales.

Parrotfishes
14 species, pg. 57

Wrasses
15 species, pg. 62

Parrotfishes, Scaridae – Most large parrotfishes are solitary, while smaller individuals regularly join loose bottom-feeding aggregations, often mixing with other species. Their scaly bodies are colored in bizarre combinations of greens and blues highlighted with reds and yellows. Several species have the ability to change colors, becoming drab, mottled or pale. Like closely related wrasses, parrotfishes swim about reefs using their pectoral fins to skillfully maneuver about bottom structures—tails are used only for bursts of speed.

Their "beaks", fused tooth plates, are used to scrape filamentous algae from the porous skeletons of dead coral rock. In the process, large amounts of coral (limestone) are taken in and ground by bony teeth plates to extract bits of plant material. On average, nearly 75 percent of the gut content of parrotfishes is composed of inorganic sediment. In fact, many divers first notice parrotfishes because of their rather unpleasant habit of voiding long plumes of excavated waste as they swim. Identification of parrotfishes is made difficult due to the dramatic changes in shape, color and markings that occur in most species as they mature. The phases include JUVENILE PHASE, INITIAL PHASE, and TERMINAL PHASE, which are the largest and most colorful, and least numerous representatives of a species.

Wrasses, Labridae – Wrasses are prolific reef inhabitants, closely related and similar to parrotfishes, but are generally much smaller, typically having more elongate "cigar" shapes, and having noticeable front teeth to seize invertebrates. By day, wrasses swim busily about the bottom in loose, often mixed aggregations. The plankton-feeding Creole Wrasse is the only family member that schools in open water.

Like parrotfishes, wrasses go through several changes in color, shape and markings during maturation. The phases include JUVENILE PHASE, INITIAL PHASE and TERMINAL PHASE, the largest and most colorful. The initial phase includes sexually mature females and, in some species, immature and mature males. All in the terminal phase are sexually mature males. Some wrasses are hermaphroditic and go through a sex reversal to become terminal phase, while others simply mature into adulthood without changing their sex. Hogfishes and razorfishes are also members of the wrasse family, but because of their unique shape have acquired separate common names. Hogfishes have long snouts which they use to root for food, similar to their namesakes. Sand-dwelling razorfishes have highly compressed "razorlike" heads used to dive beneath the sand when threatened.

STOPLIGHT PARROTFISH
Sparisoma viride
Parrotfishes – Scaridae
SIZE: 1-1½ ft., max. 2 ft.
ID: TERMINAL PHASE – Bright yellow spot at upper corner of gill cover. Emerald green. Salmon to yellow markings on head and fins. Tail is crescent-shaped. Yellow area at base of tail with salmon to yellow crescent. Swim about reefs; stop to scrape algae from rocks with stout beaks. **RANGE:** Common to occasional Caribbean, Bahamas, S. Florida.

Stoplight Parrotfish – Initial Phase   SIZE: 5-12 in.
ID: Red belly and tail. Upper body and head mottled reddish brown, often mixed with white dark bordered scales; white and red crescent on tail.

Stoplight Parrotfish – Juvenile   SIZE: 2-6 in.
ID: Three rows of widely spaced white spots run length of body.

QUEEN PARROTFISH   *Scarus vetula*
SIZE: 1-1½ ft., max. 2 ft.   Parrotfishes – Scaridae
ID: TERMINAL PHASE – Dramatic blue to green markings around mouth. Green to blue-green. May have yellow markings around mouth and stripe at base of dorsal and anal fins; tail may have light crescent marking. **RANGE:** Common to occasional Caribbean, Bahamas, S. Florida.

Queen Parrotfish – Initial Phase   SIZE: 2½-12 in.
ID: Dark gray to black. **Broad, white stripe, with diffuse edges, at midbody.**

57

Parrotfishes

PRINCESS PARROTFISH   *Scarus taeniopterus*
SIZE: 8-10 in., max. 13 in.   Parrotfishes – Scaridae
ID: TERMINAL PHASE – Borders of tail yellow to orange or pink. Blue to green; two blue to green stripes extend from snout and pass across eye. Yellow or orangish stripe down midbody, fading toward rear. **RANGE:** Common to occasional Caribbean, Bahamas, S. Florida.

Princess Parrotfish – Juvenile/Initial Phase   **SIZE:** 2-4 in.
ID: Borders of tail dark. Nose dark, never yellowish. (Similar Striped Parrotfish [next] distinguished by lack of markings on borders of tail.) White with three dark stripes on back from snout thhrough eye to tail and from chin to tail.

STRIPED PARROTFISH   *Scarus iseri*
SIZE: 8-9 in., max. 10 in.   Parrotfishes – Scaridae
ID: TERMINAL PHASE – Dark blue or green tail has pink, yellow linear markings between bluish borders. Blue to green. Gold to yellow stripe above and behind pectoral fin. **RANGE:** Abundant to common Caribbean, Bahamas, S. Florida.

Striped Parrotfish – Juvenile/Initial Phase   **SIZE:** 2-4 in.
ID: No dark marking on borders of tail. (Similar Princess Parrotfish [previous] distinguished by dark borders on tail.) White with dark back and two black stripes, white belly, often with thin, broken silver, yellow or dark stripes. Usually yellow smudge on nose; occasionally yellow wash on ventral fins, belly or tail.

REDTAIL PARROTFISH   *Sparisoma chrysopterum*
SIZE: 14-16 in., max. 18 in.   Parrotfishes – Scaridae
ID: TERMINAL PHASE – Turquoise to blue area behind pectoral fin. Olive to green to bluish green; fins often shades of red to yellow. White crescent bordered with red on tail. Pectoral fins clear with black blotch at base. **RANGE:** Common to occasional Caribbean, Bahamas, S. Florida.

Redtail Parrotfish – Initial Phase   **SIZE:** 8-14 in.
ID: Yellowish tints on tail. Reddish gray to reddish brown. Can rapidly change to pale shades of gray to brown with only tints of red around pectoral fin and gill cover. In this phase the Redtail is difficult to distinguish from IP Yellowtail Parrotfish [next] in a similar phase.

YELLOWTAIL PARROTFISH   *Sparisoma rubripinne*
SIZE: 8-14 in, max. 1½ ft.   Parrotfishes – Scaridae
ID: **TERMINAL PHASE – Central tail yellow to white with translucent margin.** May be somewhat mottled; belly often lighter shades of green to blue-green. Basal two-thirds of pectoral fin dusky with black blotch at base. **RANGE:** Common to occasional Caribbean, Bahamas, S. Florida.

Yellowtail Parrotfish – Initial Phase   SIZE: 3-9 in.
ID: **Base of tail and tail pale to bright yellow.** Mottled to solid shades of gray to brown; ventral and anal fins reddish to pink. Can rapidly change to pale shades of gray to brown or tan with no yellow on tail. In this phase the Yellowtail is difficult to distinguish from IP Redtail Parrotfish [previous] when in a similar phase.

REDBAND PARROTFISH   *Sparisoma aurofrenatum*
SIZE: 6-10 in., max. 11 in.   Parrotfishes – Scaridae
ID: **TERMINAL PHASE – Salmon to orange or yellow band from corner of mouth to below eye.** Greenish overall, underside lighter; anal fin usually reddish. Small yellow blotch with small black spots on upper forebody. **RANGE:** Abundant to common Caribbean, Bahamas, S. Florida.

Redband Parrotfish – Initial Phase Variation   SIZE: 3-6 in.
ID: **White spot behind dorsal fin present in all IP variations.** Variable with emerald body and reddish fins.

Redband Parrotfish – Initial Phase Variation   SIZE: 3-6 in.
ID: Often mottled gray to browns with two broad white stripes. Can rapidly fade, intensify or change colors and markings. White spot behind dorsal fin.

Redband Parrotfish – Juvenile   SIZE: 1½ -3 in.
ID: Shades of red-brown, usually with two white stripes and **black blotch behind upper gill cover**. White spot behind dorsal fin.

Parrotfishes

GREENBLOTCH PARROTFISH   *Sparisoma atomarium*
SIZE: 3½-4 in., max. 4½ in.   Parrotfishes – Scaridae
ID: Yellow-gold to red iris. **TERMINAL PHASE [top]** –
Shades of green to blue-green with red highlights. **INITIAL PHASE [below]** – Red overall. Usually inhabit depths below 50 ft. **RANGE:** Occasional Caribbean, Bahamas, S. Florida.

Greenblotch Parrotfish – Juvenile   **SIZE:** 1½-3½ in.
ID: Upper head has yellow-gold wash; upper body brown to yellowish red, with thin stripes below; belly white. All phases can fade, intensify or change color and markings rapidly.

BUCKTOOTH PARROTFISH   *Sparisoma radians*
SIZE: 3-5 in., max. 7½ in.   Parrotfish – Scaridae
ID: **TERMINAL PHASE – Black margin on tail and anal fin.** Highly variable combinations of mottling, blotches, patches and stripes in shades of green and earthtones. Black blotch on pectoral fin base. Inhabit seagrass. **RANGE:** Common to occasional Caribbean, Bahamas, S. Florida.

Bucktooth Parrotfish – Initial Phase   **SIZE:** 2-4 in.
ID: Bluish to greenish pectoral fin base. Colors and markings vary, often with greenish brown back and broad stripe below. Can become mottled, change color and markings rapidly to match most backgrounds.

BLUELIP PARROTFISH   *Cryptotomus roseus*
SIZE: 2½-3½ in., max. 5 in.   Parrotfishes – Scaridae
ID: TERMINAL PHASE – Broad stripe from eye to tail. Generally shades of green to blue. Display brilliant yellow or orange when reproductively active. Inhabit seagrass or nearby areas. **RANGE:** Occasional Caribbean, Bahamas, S. Florida.

Bluelip Parrotfish – Initial Phase   **SIZE:** 2½-3½ in.
ID: Slender. **Broad stripe from eye to tail.** Usually pale undercolor with stripes in shades of green-brown to reddish brown or dark brown, occasionally somewhat mottled.

EMERALD PARROTFISH *Nicholsina usta*
SIZE: 4-10 in., max. 1 ft. Parrotfishes – Scaridae
ID: TERMINAL PHASE – Narrow reddish stripe from corner of mouth to eye. Upper head green, underside whitish to yellow-green to bright yellow; upper body green; lower body pale green to rosy. **RANGE:** Uncommon to rare Caribbean, S. Florida; not reported Bahamas.

MIDNIGHT PARROTFISH *Scarus coelestinus*
SIZE: 1-2 ft., max. 3 ft. Parrotfishes – Scaridae
ID: TERMINAL PHASE – Navy blue body and fins commonly many scales have light blue centers. **Light blue markings on head.** All phases essentially the same in appearance. **RANGE:** Occasional Caribbean, Bahamas, S. Florida.

RAINBOW PARROTFISH *Scarus guacamaia*
SIZE: 1½ -3 ft., max. 4 ft. Parrotfishes – Scaridae
ID: TERMINAL PHASE – Orange-brown head. With age head becomes blunter and tips of tail grow longer. The amount of orange-brown versus green on TP varies between individuals. **RANGE:** Occasional Caribbean, Bahamas, S. Florida.

Rainbow Parrotfish – Initial Phase **SIZE:** 1-2 ft.
ID: Scale centers shades of green, edges orangish. Square cut tail. Typically inhabit areas of mangroves.

BLUE PARROTFISH *Scarus coeruleus*
SIZE: 1-2½ ft., max. 4 ft. Parrotfishes – Scaridae
ID: TERMINAL PHASE – Squared-off head. Vary from powder blue to deep blue and blue-green. **INITIAL PHASE –** Conical head. **RANGE:** Occasional Caribbean, Bahamas, S. Florida.

Blue Parrotfish – Juvenile **SIZE:** 3-10 in.
ID: Yellow wash on snout extending back to foredorsal fin. Yellow wash disappears with maturity. Bluish white to purplish blue. Some have yellow dorsal, ventral and anal fins.

Wrasses

YELLOWHEAD WRASSE
Halichoeres garnoti
Wrasses – Labridae
SIZE: 5-6 in., max. 8 in.
ID: TERMINAL PHASE – Yellow head and forebody. Head and forebody vary from bright yellow to yellowish or greenish tan. Dark midbody bar continues as a wide border along back to dark tail. Two wavy lines radiate from rear upper eye. **RANGE:** Common Caribbean, Bahamas, S. Florida.

Yellowhead Wrasse – Initial Phase **SIZE:** 3-5 in.
ID: Dark to dusky back, often shaded with blue. Body and undersides highly variable in colors ranging from bright yellow to green an blue-green.

Yellowhead Wrasse – Initial Phase **SIZE:** 3-5 in.
ID: All IP color phases have the distinctive two wavy lines radiating from the rear upper eye. Color shadings highly variable, especially intermediates between IP and juveniles.

Yellowhead Wrasse – Juvenile **SIZE:** 1-3 in.
ID: Usually bright yellow with a brilliant blue midbody stripe.

Yellowhead Wrasse – Juvenile **SIZE:** 1-3 in.
ID: Juveniles on rare occasions display reddish gold shading.

BLUEHEAD
Thalassoma bifasciatum
Wrasses – Labridae
SIZE: 4-5 in., max. 6 in.
ID: TERMINAL PHASE – Blue head. Two dark bands behind head separated by white V-shaped bar. Rear body green to blue-green. **RANGE:** Abundant to common Caribbean, Bahamas, S. Florida.

Bluehead – Transitional Phase   **SIZE:** 3-5 in.
ID: Broad dark bands interspersed with white appear during transition from IP to TP.

Bluehead – Juvenile/Initial Phase   **SIZE:** 1½-3 in.
ID: Black spot behind second dorsal ray. IP and juveniles cannot be distinguished by color pattern or size. they display three basic patterns, all with white belly. A yellow body and white belly with vague black markings is by far the most common pattern.

Bluehead – Juvenile/Initial Phase   **SIZE:** 1½-3 in.
ID: IP and juveniles often display a broad, dark midbody stripe that runs from snout to tail base. IP individuals as small as 1½ inches can be sexually mature females or males. In areas with large Bluehead populations groups of IP individuals, numbering in the hundreds, gather to group spawn in the water column.

Bluehead – Juvenile/Initial Phase   **SIZE:** 1½-3 in.
ID: In some regions a few individuals do not display any yellow. Juveniles often act as cleaners, removing parasites from larger fish. Schools numbering a dozen or more often swim about feeding.

SLIPPERY DICK
Halichoeres bivittatus
Wrasses – Labridae
SIZE: 5¹/₂-7 in., max. 9 in.
ID: ALL PHASES – Small green and yellow bicolored spot above pectoral fin. Darkish to black midbody stripe; a second, lower stripe is less distinct (often absent in juveniles). **TERMINAL PHASE –** Shades of green with dark triangular corners on tail. Tend to be more secretive than other family members; use elongate mouth to probe deep recesses for marine invertebrates. **RANGE:** Common Caribbean, Bahamas, S. Florida.

Slippery Dick – Initial Phase   **SIZE:** 3-6 in.
ID: Display shades of green to brown with vague dark midbody stripe, a second lower stripe and dark bars on back occasionally extending to underside.

Slippery Dick – Juvenile   **SIZE:** 1¹/₂-3 in.
ID: White with a dark stripe down center of body. White quickly changes to tan or brown when individual swim over dark bottom features. Most individuals have a small dark spot at the rear base of the pectoral fin; many young IP display a small black spot or large blue dot on middorsal fin.

BLACKEAR WRASSE   *Halichoeres poeyi*
SIZE: 4-5¹/₂ in., max. 8 in.   Wrasses – Labridae
ID: ALL PHASES – Small, orange to purplish red spot upper rear of eye. Black spot at base of rear dorsal fin. **TERMINAL PHASE –** Shades of green to purplish brown, often with orangish shading on forebody. Reddish diagonal "V" on tail.
RANGE: Occasional Caribbean, Bahamas, S. Florida.

Blackear Wrasse – Juvenile   **SIZE:** 2-4 in.
ID: Shades of green to chartreuse with dark bars. Dark spot on dorsal fin.

CLOWN WRASSE
Halichoeres maculipinna
Wrasses – Labridae
SIZE: 3-5 in., max. 6½ in.

ID: TERMINAL PHASE – Two dark spots on foredorsal fin merge to form an elongate oval. A variety of markings and shadings in green, blue, violet, rose, orange and yellow. Commonly display a dark midbody blotch. Often reddish highlights on the tail. **RANGE:** Occasional Caribbean, Bahamas, S. Florida.

Clown Wrasse – Initial Phase　　　**SIZE:** 3-4 in.

ID: Two dark spots on foredorsal fin. Three red line markings across top of head and two U-shaped lines on snout are also present in the TP. Often have a pale belly.

Clown Wrasse – Juvenile　　　**SIZE:** 1½ -3 in.

ID: Thin yellow-gold stripe runs from snout, above eye, to tail, with a wider black stripe below and a pale belly.

RAINBOW WRASSE　　　*Halichoeres pictus*
SIZE: 2-2¾ in., max. 3 in.　　　Wrasses – Labridae

ID: TERMINAL PHASE – Black blotch on base of tail. Green to blue green to gold upper body, pale underside with darkish stripe from eye to tail base. Typically swim well above bottom. **RANGE:** Common to occasional Caribbean, Bahamas; rare S. Florida.

Rainbow Wrasse – Juvenile　　　**SIZE:** 1½ -2 in.

ID: Black stripe on top of head runs from above eye to dorsal fin. Golden body with broad dusky red midbody stripe extending from dark stripe through eye to tail. Often cluster in groups with other small fishes on deeper slopes and walls. **INITIAL PHASE –** Similar Juvenile/IP Bluehead and Wrasse Blenny distinguished by black spot on foredorsal fin.

65

YELLOWCHEEK WRASSE   *Halichoeres cyanocephalus*
SIZE: 3-6 in., max. 12 in.   Wrasses – Labridae
ID: **TERMINAL PHASE – Two wavy lines radiate from upper rear of eye.** All phases have yellow wash running from mouth across nape to foredorsal fin, with broad blue area below. Inhabit patch reefs below 50 ft. **RANGE:** Uncommon to rare Caribbean, S. Florida; absent Bahamas.

Yellowcheek Wrasse – Juvenile   SIZE: 1½-3 in.
ID: **Deep blue spot on middorsal fin and another on base of tail.** Broad area of blue to tan stretches from eye to tail.

PUDDINGWIFE   *Halichoeres radiatus*
SIZE: 12-15 in., max. 18 in.   Wrasses – Labridae
ID: **TERMINAL PHASE –** Shades of green to orange with pale to bright yellow margin on tail. Scrawled pattern on head and occasionally broad white midbody bar. TP rare compared to the IP. **RANGE:** Common to occasional Caribbean, Bahamas, S. Florida.

Puddingwife – Initial Phase   SIZE: 6-12 in.
ID: Shades of green to orange **often with four white saddle markings across back.** Constantly stay on the move.

Puddingwife – Juvenile   SIZE: 1-3 in.
ID: Yellowish green to bluish green with areas of yellow gold; **large round to oval black spot on middorsal fin extends onto back and another roundish dark spot on upper base of tail.** Reddish highlight on dorsal and anal fins. Typically inhabit patch reefs in shallow areas.

DWARF WRASSE   *Doratonotus megalepis*
SIZE: 1½-2½ in., max. 3 in.   Wrasses – Labridae
ID: **Foredorsal fin (first three spines) tall and distinct.** Vary from green to tan with scattered white, yellowish to reddish markings. Pointed snout. May display bars. Can change color and pale or darken. Inhabit seagrass beds. **RANGE:** Rare Caribbean, Bahamas, S. Florida.

CREOLE WRASSE
Clepticus parrae
Wrasse – Labridae
SIZE: 4-7 in., max. 1 ft.

ID: TERMINAL PHASE – Variable combinations of blue forebody with yellow and purple blotching on rear and tail. **Yellow area on some portion of rear body.** Feed on plankton along deep, outer reefs, especially the edges of drop-offs. Swim constantly, often in open water above reefs, in small groups to large schools. Commonly form long streaming schools along drop-offs where they pair up to spawn daily from mid- to late-afternoon. Frequently attend cleaning stations. **RANGE:** Abundant Caribbean; common Bahamas, S. Florida.

Creole Wrasse – Initial Phase   **SIZE:** 3-6 in.
ID: Dark purple to violet or lavender. Dark mask on snout also present on TP.

Creole Wrasse – Juvenile   **SIZE:** 1-2 in.
ID: Series of spots or short bands along back composed of dark and light dots. Often gather in clusters along reef slopes.

SPANISH HOGFISH   *Bodianus rufus*
SIZE: 8-14 in., max. 2 ft.   Hogfishes/Wrasses – Labridae
ID: ALL PHASES – Purplish upper forebody with yellow belly and tail. TP can only be distinguished from IP by their larger size. **RANGE:** Common Caribbean, Bahamas, S. Florida.

SPOTFIN HOGFISH   *Bodianus pulchellus*
SIZE: 4½ - 7½ in., max.9 in.   Hogfishes/Wrasses – Labridae
ID: Yellow tail and base. TP red, IP blackish; both with white streak from under eye onto body. **RANGE:** Common Florida; occasional Bahamas, uncommon Caribbean..

HOGFISH
Lachnolaimus maximus
Hogfishes/Wrasses – Labridae
SIZE: 1-2 ft., max. 3 ft.
ID: TERMINAL PHASE – Have pronounced upturned snout and wide dark bar across tail. Vary from pearl white to mottled or banded reddish brown; large, dusky to dark area covering snout and nape to foredorsal fin. First three spines of dorsal fin are long. Most common on open bottoms, occasionally on reefs. Swim constantly; occasionally stopping to dig in search of food. **RANGE:** Common S. Florida; occasional Caribbean, Bahamas.

Hogfish – Intermediate Phase   **SIZE:** 1-2 ft.
ID: Less pronounced snout shaded with light brown; **black blotch on base of rear dorsal fin.**

Hogfish – Intermediate Phase   **SIZE:** 1-2 ft.
ID: Individuals often display a dramatic reddish mottled pattern when near bottom or attending cleaning station.

ROSY RAZORFISH   *Xyrichtys martinicensis*
SIZE: 3-4 1/2 in., max. 6 in.   Razorfishes/Wrasses – Labridae
ID: MALE – Dark blotch at base of pectoral fin. Mixture of pastel green, blue and yellow; head usually pale yellow with faint bars. Inhabit inshore sand areas. **RANGE:** Common to occasional Caribbean, Bahamas, S. Florida.

Rosy Razorfish – Female   **SIZE:** 2 1/2-3 1/2 in., max. 4 1/2 in.
ID: White belly patch with reddish line markings and darkish bar on gill cover. Pearl white head with grayish to rosy-pearl body. Brownish body stripe with vague bars lost with maturity. Hover above sandy areas, often near or in seagrass. If alarmed, can dive into the sand and occasionally tunnel underneath for some distance. Head reappears a few minutes later.

GREEN RAZORFISH
Xyrichtys splendens
Razorfishes/Wrasses – Labridae
SIZE: 2½-4 in., max. 5½ in.

ID: MALE – Have a dark spot (occasionally two) at midbody. Colors vary, but generally have greenish cast. Often have bars and markings ranging from reddish brown to yellow, green and white; reddish dorsal and anal fins. Thin line markings on gill cover. Margin of tail rounded. Hover above shallow, sandy bottoms, often near rocks, gorgonians or other cover. Often hover with curled body in slightly head up position. If alarmed, can dive into the sand and tunnel underneath for some distance. Head reappears a few minutes later. **RANGE:** Occasional Caribbean, Bahamas, S. Florida.

Green Razorfish – Female   **SIZE:** 1½-3 in., max 4 in.
ID: Highly variable color from shades of green to orange, yellow and brown, often with bar markings. High foredorsal fin.

Green Razorfish – Juvenile   **SIZE:** ¾-1½ in.
ID: First two dorsal spines are long, with pigmented tissue between. Clear dorsal fin with two or three pigmented bars.

PEARLY RAZORFISH   *Xyrichtys novacula*
SIZE: 5-10 in., max. 15 in.   Razorfishes/Wrasses – Labridae
ID: MALE – Wide, diagonal, dusky or reddish band on side. Typically pearly white, often with tints of blue to green, rose, orange or brown. Steep head profile. Dive into sand when alarmed. **RANGE:** Uncommon Caribbean, Bahamas, S. Florida.

Pearly Razorfish – Female   **SIZE:** 5-8 in., max. 10 in.
ID: Typically pearly white unmarked body, often with tints of blue or green, rose, orange or brown.

Reddish/Big Eyes
Cardinalfishes – Squirrelfishes – Bigeyes

This ID Group consists of night-feeding fishes that range in color from pale red to reddish brown and have large eyes.

Squirrelfishes
7 species, pg. 71

Bigeyes
2 species, pg. 72

Cardinalfishes
18 species, pg. 73

Squirrelfishes, Holocentridae – This family of reddish fishes, with large "squirrellike" eyes and a long, pronounced rear dorsal fin that sticks up in a way reminiscent of a squirrel's tail, is among the most striking on the reef. Family member display thin, white, or occasionally yellow-gold, body stripes (with the exception of soldierfishes). Although nocturnal, most may be sighted hiding within the shadows of the reef during the day. After sunset squirrelfishes migrate away from the reef to forage for crabs and shrimps on sand flats and seagrass beds.

Occasionally the typically solitary squirrelfish species gather in loose groups near the entrances of large reef pockets. Family members are similar in appearance, but each species has a distinctive feature that make identification easy. Juvenile squirrelfishes are thin, silvery pelagics, and are seldom seen.

Bigeyes, Priacanthidae – Bigeyes and Glasseye Snappers are the only members of this family commonly found shallower than 130 feet. These generally solitary family members have large eyes and continuous dorsal fins. Both species can lighten their red coloration considerably. The night-foraging carnivores feed primarily on larval forms of fishes and crustaceans.

Cardinalfishes, Apogonidae – Cardinalfishes are named for their typically reddish color. They are quite small (one to three inches), have large eyes, relatively short snouts, and two separate dorsal fins. Although common reef inhabitants, the nocturnal feeders are seldom sighted by divers because they hide during the day in protected recesses of the reef. Large groups of cardinalfishes are occasionally found inside caves. A few species live in association with invertebrates such as tube sponges, anemones and Queen Conch. At night they feed several feet above the bottom on larval shrimps, crabs and copepods suspended in the water. The males of several species incubate eggs inside their mouths. Black spots, dark body bars, eye markings, and their association with invertebrates are the keys to species identification.

SQUIRRELFISH
Holocentrus adscensionis
Squirrelfishes – Holocentridae
SIZE: 6-12 in., max. 16 in.
ID: Yellowish front dorsal fin. Reddish with light silvery stripes and occasional white patches on body. Elongate rear dorsal fin and lobes of tail. Largest squirrelfish. Nocturnal; during day, drift inconspicuously in shaded areas near bottom. Most abundant on shallow patch reefs and wall tops. Occasionally gather in groups. **RANGE:** Common Caribbean, Bahamas; occasional S. Florida.

LONGSPINE SQUIRRELFISH   *Holocentrus rufus*
SIZE: 5-10 in., max. 12½ in.   Squirrelfishes – Holocentridae
ID: White triangular markings at tips of dorsal fin spines. Reddish with light silvery stripes and white patches on body. Elongate rear dorsal fin and tail lobes. **RANGE:** Common Caribbean, Bahamas; occasional S. Florida.

REEF SQUIRRELFISH   *Sargocentron coruscum*
SIZE: 3½-5 in., max. 5½ in.   Squirrelfishes – Holocentridae
ID: Black blotch on first dorsal fin runs from first spine to third or fourth spine. Reddish with light silvery body stripes. Tips and base of front dorsal fin marked with white. **RANGE:** Uncommon Caribbean, Bahamas, S. Florida.

DUSKY SQUIRRELFISH   *Sargocentron vexillarium*
SIZE: 3-5 in., max. 7 in.   Squirrelfishes – Holocentridae
ID: Anal and tail fins bordered in brownish red to bright red. Usually dusky, bronze-red (occasionally orange to gold or silver) stripes alternate with wide silver stripes. Inhabit crevices in shallow rocky coasts and reef crests. **RANGE:** Occasional Caribbean, Bahamas, S. Florida.

LONGJAW SQUIRRELFISH   *Neoniphon marianus*
SIZE: 4-6 in., max. 7 in.   Squirrelfishes – Holocentridae
ID: Orangish gold body stripes. Silvery red. Gold front dorsal fin patterned with white tips and spots along base. Unusually long anal fin spine. Usually below 50 ft. **RANGE:** Common Caribbean, Bahamas; uncommon S. Florida.

BLACKBAR SOLDIERFISH *Myripristis jacobus*
SIZE: 4-6 in., max. 8½ in.   Squirrelfishes – Holocentridae
ID: Black bar behind head. Bright red to, on rare occasions, pale red. Red dorsal fin has white marks at tips and a few along base. White borders on leading edge of ventral, anal, rear dorsal and tail fins. Often gather in large schools. **RANGE:** Common to occasional Caribbean, Bahamas, S. Florida.

CARDINAL SOLDIERFISH *Plectrypops retrospinis*
SIZE: 4-6 in., max. 8½ in.   Squirrelfishes – Holocentridae
ID: Lobes of tail rounded. Unmarked bright red to orangish red. Fins may be pale; belly occasionally lighter shades of red. Reclusive and wary. **RANGE:** Occasional eastern Caribbean; uncommon remainder of Caribbean, Bahamas, S. Florida.

BIGEYE
Priacanthus arenatus
Bigeyes – Priacanthidae
SIZE: 8-12 in., max. 16 in.
ID: Uniform reddish color. Vary from bright red to salmon; often have blackish tinges. No markings other than possible duskiness along edges of rear dorsal, anal and tail fins. May pale to almost white and display dark red area beneath eye. Usually solitary, but occasionally form loose groups. Generally prefer deep reef tops. Easily approached. **RANGE:** Occasional Caribbean, Bahamas, S. Florida.

GLASSEYE SNAPPER *Heteropriacanthus cruentatus*
SIZE: 7-10 in, max. 1 ft.   Bigeyes – Priacanthidae
ID: Always display silver bars on back, which may be faint. Vary from red to pale, silvery or mottled pink. Often hide in dark recesses of reefs by day, but occasionally drift in open near bottom. Generally prefer shallow reefs. **RANGE:** Common to occasional Caribbean, Bahamas, S. Florida.

Glasseye Snapper – Juvenile   **SIZE:** 2-6 in.
ID: Mottled with black and white markings on tan undercolor. Translucent fins with dark spots.

BELTED CARDINALFISH
Apogon townsendi
Cardinalfishes – Apogonidae
SIZE: 1¼-2 in., max. 2½ in.

ID: Dark bar from rear dorsal fin to anal fin and **two bars at base of tail (may have darkish area between bars forming one wide bar with dark borders).** Orangish red with yellowish belly. Hide by day in dark recesses. Feed in the open on reefs at night. **RANGE:** Common Caribbean, Bahamas; uncommon S. Florida.

BARRED CARDINALFISH *Apogon binotatus*
SIZE: 1½-3½ in., max. 4½ in.   Cardinalfishes – Apogonidae
ID: Black bar from rear dorsal to anal fin and **single black bar at base of tail.** Deep orangish red or bronze to pink or salmon; can pale dramatically. Nocturnal. **RANGE:** Common to occasional Caribbean, Bahamas, S. Florida.

MIMIC CARDINALFISH *Apogon phenax*
SIZE: 1½-2½ in., max. 3 in.   Cardinalfishes – Apogonidae
ID: Dark triangular bar below rear end of second dorsal fin (the bar in this position on all similar appearing species is never triangular). Pinkish red with broad bar on base of tail. Nocturnal. **RANGE:** Uncommon Caribbean, Bahamas, S. Florida.

ROUGHLIP CARDINALFISH *Apogon robinsi*
SIZE: 1½-3½ in., max. 4 in.   Cardinalfishes – Apogonidae
ID: Darkish red areas along base of rear dorsal and anal fins, and on borders of tail. Dusky bar extends from below rear dorsal fin to belly (never triangular). **RANGE:** Uncommon Bahamas, northwestern Caribbean; not reported S. Florida or balance of Caribbean.

PALE CARDINALFISH *Apogon planifrons*
SIZE: 1½-3½ in., max. 4 in.   Cardinalfishes – Apogonidae
ID: Dark bar extends from below rear dorsal fin to belly (never triangular). Dusky bar at base of tail (wider than bar on similar Barred Cardinalfish [above left]). Often display pearly highlights. **RANGE:** Uncommon Caribbean, Bahamas, S. Florida.

Cardinalfishes

FLAMEFISH
Apogon maculatus
Cardinalfishes – Apogonidae
SIZE: 2-3¹/₂ in., max. 4¹/₂ in.
ID: **Two white lines across eye. Dark blotch behind eye.** Bright red to salmon. Usually have black spot below rear dorsal fin; darkish streak may run from eye to rear of gill cover; faint bar on base of tail occasionally present.
RANGE: Common to occasional Caribbean, Bahamas, S. Florida.

Flamefish – Variation
ID: Pale variation without spot below rear dorsal fin or bar on tail base.

Flamefish – Variation
ID: Bright red variation without bar on tail base.

TWOSPOT CARDINALFISH   *Apogon pseudomaculatus*
SIZE: 1¹/₂-3 in., max. 4¹/₂ in.   Cardinalfishes – Apogonidae
ID: **Dark spot on back under rear dorsal fin and second dark spot at base of tail.** (Similar Flamefish [previous] does not have a spot on base of tail, but may have dark bar.)
RANGE: Uncommon Caribbean, Bahamas, S. Florida.

BROADSADDLE CARDINALFISH   *Apogon pillionatus*
SIZE: 1¹/₂-2 in., max. 2¹/₂ in.   Cardinalfishes – Apogonidae
ID: **Wide dark saddle on base of tail with white bar behind** (may display a second white bar in front of saddle [pictured]). Bar below rear of second dorsal fin does not reach lower edge of body. **RANGE:** Uncommon Caribbean, Bahamas, S. Florida.

SAWCHEEK CARDINALFISH *Apogon quadrisquamatus*
SIZE: 1¹/₂-2 in., max. 2¹/₂ in.　Cardinalfishes – Apogonidae
ID: Dusky band at base of tail. Bright red to bronze to salmon. Often dusky, wedge-shaped mark adjacent to lower rear eye; indistinct body stripes may run to base of tail. **RANGE:** Occasional Caribbean, Bahamas, S. Florida.

STRIPED CARDINALFISH *Apogon robbyi*
SIZE: 1-1¹/₄ in., max. 1¹/₂ in.　Cardinalfishes – Apogonidae
ID: About seven pale body stripes. Bright red to reddish orange to pale orange; fins translucent often with pale to bright yellow tints. Often large dark to dusky spot on tail base. **RANGE:** Occasional Belize, Cayman, Jamaica, Isla Providencia and San Andres, but probably have a wider range.

BIGTOOTH CARDINALFISH *Apogon affinis*
SIZE: 1¹/₂-3 in., max. 4 in.　Cardinalfishes – Apogonidae
ID: Dusky stripe across eye. Translucent salmon to pink or bronze; clear fins. Lower jaw juts out extending beyond the upper jaw. Often in large aggregations. **RANGE:** Uncommon Caribbean, Bahamas, S. Florida.

ODDSCALE CARDINALFISH *Apogon evermanni*
SIZE: 1¹/₂-2 in., max. 2¹/₂ in.　Cardinalfishes – Apogonidae
ID: Black spot at base of last dorsal fin rays and white spot behind. Dusky to black stripe extends from behind eye to edge of gill cover. (Whitestar Cardinalfish [next] lacks this marking.) May display pale bars. **RANGE:** Uncommon in Bahamas and scattered locations in Caribbean including Cozumel.

WHITESTAR CARDINALFISH
Apogon lachneri
Cardinalfishes – Apogonidae
SIZE: 1¹/₂-2¹/₂ in., max. 3 in.
ID: Brilliant white spot just behind small, dark blotch on back, behind dorsal fin. Bright red to salmon. (Lacks dusky to black stripe through eye like Oddscale Cardinalfish [previous]). **RANGE:** Occasional Caribbean, Bahamas; uncommon S. Florida.

Cardinalfishes

BRIDLE CARDINALFISH   *Apogon aurolineatus*
SIZE: 1¹/₂-2¹/₄ in., max. 2¹/₂ in.   Cardinalfishes – Apogonidae
ID: Thin line "bridle" extends from upper rear eye and a second line from below eye. Bright red to bronze to salmon. Live with anemones. **RANGE:** Uncommon Caribbean, Bahamas, S. Florida.

FRECKLED CARDINALFISH   *Phaeoptyx conklini*
SIZE: 1¹/₂-3 in., max. 3¹/₂ in.   Cardinalfishes – Apogonidae
ID: Dusky bar on upper first doral fin and another above base of second dorsal. Pinkish to reddish with rows of dark rectangular spots on body. **RANGE:** Occasional Caribbean, Bahamas, S. Florida.

DUSKY CARDINALFISH   *Phaeoptyx pigmentaria*
SIZE: 1¹/₂-3 in., max. 3 in.   Cardinalfishes – Apogonidae
ID: Dorsal and anal fins transparent without markings. Pinkish to reddish with rows of small dark round spots on body; dark bar on base of tail. **RANGE:** Occasional Florida, Bahamas, Caribbean.

CONCHFISH   *Astrapogon stellatus*
SIZE: 1-2 in., max. 3 in.   Cardinalfishes – Apogonidae
ID: Mottled, pale grayish bronze to black. No distinguishing marks. Numerous black speckles. Often two to four broad streaks radiate from eyes. Dark, elongate ventral fin. Inhabit mantle cavity of living Queen Conch. **RANGE:** Uncommon Caribbean, Bahamas, S. Florida.

BLACKFIN CARDINALFISH
Astrapogon puncticulatus
Cardinalfishes – Apogonidae
SIZE: 1-2 in., max. 2¹/₂ in.
ID: Large, dramatic ventral fin usually with dark leading edge. Bronze cast, with numerous black and white speckles, often with bluish, goldish or greenish highlights. Usually have pearly patch behind and below eye. Blunt, rounded snout. Inhabit seagrass beds in clear water. **RANGE:** Uncommon Caribbean, Bahamas, S. Florida.

Small, Elongated Bottom-Dwellers
Gobies – Blennies – Dragonets – Jawfishes

This ID Group consists of fishes that that generally grow to no more than three inches. All have long, cylindrical bodies and spend most of their time perched on the bottom or inside small holes with only their heads protruding. A few species drift just above the bottom.

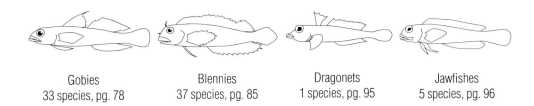

Gobies	Blennies	Dragonets	Jawfishes
33 species, pg. 78	37 species, pg. 85	1 species, pg. 95	5 species, pg. 96

Gobies, Gobidae – Gobies are small (generally one to two inches, with only a few species exceeding two and a half inches). Most rest on their pectoral and ventral fins. Some species, particularlly those inhabiting surge areas, develop a small suction disc between their ventral fins to anchor them in place. A few species drift in open water near the reef. Gobies and blennies are often confused, but can easily be distinguished by their dorsal fins — gobies have two, while most blennies have one long, continuous fin. Gobies also have a tendency to rest with stiff, straight bodies, while blennies perch in a more relaxed flexed or curved position.

Blennies – Four scientific families comprise the common group name blenny. Scaly Blennies, **Labrisomidae** have scales and a single dorsal fin; Tube Blennies, **Chaenopsidae** lack scales and a lateral line, have a single high front dorsal fin and often inhabit abandoned worm holes (tubes) in the reef; Combtooth Blennies, **Blenniidae** also lack scales, but have a lateral line and single dorsal fin; Triplefin Blennies, **Tripterygiidae** have scales and three separate dorsal fins. Most blennies are small (one to three inches) and elongate with long, thin ventral fins which they use to perch on the bottom. While resting and swimming, blennies tend to curve and flex their bodies in contrast to the gobies, which hold their bodies stiff and straight. Most blennies have fleshy appendages, called cirri, above their eyes. A few bennies also have additional cirri on their snouts and napes. Several species live in holes and are only seen with their heads exposed. Occasionally, darting out to nab a drifting particle of food. Many blennies are similar in appearance and difficult to distinguish. Adding to the confusion, males and females of several species are dramatically different in appearance.

Dragonet, Callionymidae – These tiny algae-eating bottom-dwellers are so cleverly concealed by their brown camouflage that only quick, intermittent sprints across the sand give their position away. Males are larger than the females, and also have a much higher and larger first dorsal fin.

Jawfishes, Opistognathidae – Jawfishes are named for their large mouths and gaping jaws. They live in holes which they construct by moving stones and sand with their mouths. Generally, they are seen with only their heads protruding, but on occasion they hover just above the bottom. When frightened, they rapidly retreat into the confines of the hole, usually tail first. Their bulbous heads are bulky in comparison to their elongate bodies. The jawfish family is easy to identify, but a few species are almost impossible to distinguish with only their heads visible. Jawfish males incubate eggs inside their mouths.

Gobies

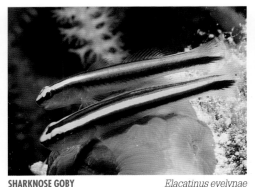

SHARKNOSE GOBY *Elacatinus evelynae*
SIZE: 1-1¼ in., max. 1½ in. Gobies – Gobiidae
ID: Three color variations. (1) [above top] Bright "V" on snout fades into pale or brilliant blue body stripes. (2) [above bottom] Yellow "V" on snout continues into yellow body stripes. **RANGE:** Common to occasional Caribbean, Bahamas; not reported S. Florida.

CAYMAN CLEANING GOBY *Elacatinus cayman*
SIZE: 1-1¼ in., max. 1½ in. Gobies – Gobiidae
ID: Bright yellow "V" on snout continues as narrow stripe to tail with white borders. Dark upper body, pale below; underslung mouth. **RANGE:** Common Cayman Islands. Not known elsewhere.

CLEANING GOBY
Elacatinus genie
Gobies – Gobiidae
SIZE: 1-1¼ in., max. 1¾ in.

ID: Brilliant yellow, occasionally white, "V" on snout fades into wide pale body stripe. Dark upper body, pale underside. Mouth is underslung. Cleaner fish. Congregate in cleaning stations where they perch in groups, waiting for client fishes requiring their services. **RANGE:** Common to occasional Bahamas, Caribbean islands; uncommon coastal Central and South America; not reported S. Florida.

NEON GOBY *Elacatinus oceanops*
SIZE: 1-1½ in., max. 2 in. Gobies – Gobiidae
ID: Electric blue body stripe runs from front of each eye to base of tail. No markings on snout. Dark upper body, pale underside. **RANGE:** Common S. Florida. Similar-appearing Caribbean Neon Goby, *E. lobeli*, occasional Belize and Honduras.

YELLOWLINE GOBY *Elacatinus horsti*
SIZE: 1-1½ in., max. 2 in. Gobies – Gobiidae
ID: Yellow or white body stripe runs from front of each eye to tail. Dark upper body, pale underside. Mouth located near tip of snout. **RANGE:** Common southern Caribbean; occasional northwestern Caribbean; uncommon to rare balance of Caribbean and Bahamas; not reported S. Florida.

SPOTLIGHT GOBY   *Elacatinus louisae*
SIZE: 1-1¹/₄ in., max. 1¹/₂ in.   Gobies – Gobiidae
ID: Bright yellow spot centered on snout. Thin yellow body stripe runs from each eye to tail. Yellow markings may pale. Dark upper body with pale underside. Mouth located near tip of snout. **RANGE:** Uncommon Bahamas and northern Caribbean; not reported southern Caribbean, S. Florida.

YELLOWPROW GOBY   *Elacatinus xanthiprora*
SIZE: 1-1¹/₄ in., max. 1¹/₂ in.   Gobies – Gobiidae
ID: Bright yellow or white bar on dark snout. Bright yellow or white body stripe runs from each eye to tail. The bar and body stripe are most often yellow, but can be white, or pale iridescent blue. **RANGE:** Uncommon to rare Caribbean, Bahamas, S. Florida.

YELLOWNOSE GOBY   *Elacatinus randalli*
SIZE: 1-1¹/₄ in., max. 1³/₄ in.   Gobies – Gobiidae
ID: Bright yellow bar on pale snout. Yellow stripe runs from each eye to tail. Thin bluish stripe runs from under each eye to behind pectoral fin. Dark upper body and pale belly. **RANGE:** Common southern Caribbean; not reported balance of Caribbean, Bahamas, S. Florida.

LINESNOUT GOBY   *Elacatinus lori*
SIZE: 1-1¹/₄ in., max. 1³/₄ in.   Gobies – Gobiidae
ID: White bar runs from upper lip to between eyes on dark upper head. Blue stripe runs from each eye to tail. Dark upper body with pale belly. Mouth located near tip of snout; tail rounded. **RANGE:** Occasional western Caribbean.

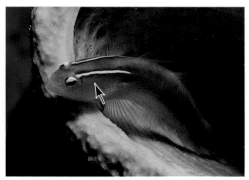

BROADSTRIPE GOBY   *Elacatinus prochilos*
SIZE: 1-1¹/₄ in., max. 1³/₄ in.   Gobies – Gobiidae
ID: White "V" or "Y" on snout continues into white or bluish white body stripes. Dark upper body, pale belly. Mouth located near tip of snout. **RANGE:** Occasional northwestern Caribbean and Lesser Antilles; Uncommon Bahamas; not reported Florida.

SHORTSTRIPE GOBY   *Elacatinus chancei*
SIZE: 1-1¹/₄ in., max. 1¹/₂ in.   Gobies – Gobiidae
ID: A short, bright yellow stripe runs from each eye to above pectoral fin. Dark upper body with pale belly. Snout and nape may be pale with yellowish or whitish cast. Mouth located near tip of snout. **RANGE:** Occasional Bahamas and eastern Caribbean; rare western Caribbean; not reported S. Florida.

Gobies

BRIDLED GOBY
Coryphopterus glaucofraenum
Gobies – Gobiidae
SIZE: 1½-2½ in., max. 3 in.
ID: In a row of about 4 white spots behind eye, second is elevated and underlined with black; white "bridle" runs from mouth to edge of gill cover with darkish band above anterior end and occasionally the entire length. Usually two dark spots on base of tail; pale to translucent body with numerous white and darker spots. **RANGE:** Abundant to common Caribbean, Bahamas, S. Florida.

SAND-CANYON GOBY *Coryphopterus bol*
SIZE: 1½-2½ in., max. 3 in. Gobies – Gobiidae
ID: Orange to brown spot on lower third of pectoral fin base. White "bridle" runs from rear of mouth to gill cover with no darkish band above. Usually below 50 ft. **RANGE:** Common Florida, Bahamas, Caribbean.

PATCH-REEF GOBY *Coryphopterus tortugae*
SIZE: 1½-2½ in., max. 3 in. Gobies – Gobiidae
ID: No orange to brown spot on lower third of pectoral fin base. White "bridle" runs from rear of mouth to gill cover with no darkish band above. **RANGE:** Common Florida, Bahamas, Caribbean.

PALLID GOBY *Coryphopterus eidolon*
SIZE: 1¼-1¾ in., max. 2 in. Gobies – Gobiidae
ID: **Yellow stripe extends from rear of eye (may have dark outline).** Translucent with dusky bar on base of tail; often faint goldish blotches or stripes on body; dusky blotch behind pectoral fin. **RANGE:** Common S. Caribbean; occasional remainder of Caribbean, Bahamas; uncommon S. Florida.

COLON GOBY *Coryphopterus dicrus*
SIZE: 1¼-1¾ in., max. 2 in. Gobies – Gobiidae
ID: **Two darkish spots in front of pectoral fin base.** White to tan translucent body. Bar at base of tail fin (may consist of two dots only lightly joined); body speckled with reddish brown spots; head may have a few dusky markings. **RANGE:** Common to occasional Caribbean, Bahamas, S. Florida.

SPOTTED GOBY *Coryphopterus punctipectophorus*
SIZE: 1¼-1¾ in., max. 2 in. Gobies – Gobiidae
ID: Dark spot at lower base of pectoral fin. Darkish stripes at top and bottom of dorsal fins with whitish stripe between. White to bluish white to translucent. Series of diffuse blotches and spots on sides. **RANGE:** Uncommon to rare Caribbean, Bahamas, S. Florida.

DASH GOBY *Ctenogobius saepepallens*
SIZE: 1-1½ in., max. 2 in. Gobies – Gobiidae
ID: Dark spot in front of pectoral fin and series of dashes behind form broken stripe along midbody. White to bluish gray, reddish brown or tan. Dark bar runs across eye and down cheek. **RANGE:** Uncommon to rare Caribbean, Bahamas, S. Florida.

WHITE-EYE GOBY *Bollmannia boqueronensis*
SIZE: 1½-3 in., max. 4 in. Gobies – Gobiidae
ID: Black spot on first dorsal fin ringed with white. White to pale translucent or transparent; head often yellowish; may have yellow to orange stripes and spots on second dorsal fin. Tail long and pointed. **RANGE:** Rare Caribbean, S. Florida; not reported Bahamas.

GOLDSPOT GOBY
Gnatholepis cauerensis
Gobies – Gobiidae
SIZE: 1½-2½ in., max. 3 in.
ID: Dark bar runs from top of head across eye and down cheek. Whitish to tan. Dusky dots and squarish blotches along lower body. Whitish to tan. Commonly a small, bright gold spot within a black patch above pectoral fin. **RANGE:** Abundant to common Caribbean, Bahamas, S. Florida.

SPOTFIN GOBY *Oxyurichthys stigmalophius*
SIZE: 3-5 in., max. 6½ in. Gobies – Gobiidae
ID: Dark spot on lower rear foredorsal fin. Whitish to pale brown or blue with four to five large spots on mid-body; occasionally orange to orangish spots and rectangular markings on upper body and head. **RANGE:** Uncommon to rare Caribbean, Bahamas, S. Florida.

Gobies

GREENBANDED GOBY *Tigrigobius harveyi*
SIZE: 1-1½ in., max. 1¾ in.
Gobies – Gobiidae
ID: Numerous (19) light green bands ring body. Red stripe starts at tip of snout and runs across eye to above pectoral fin. Fins pale green; underside of head white. Live under rocks, sea urchins and sponges in shallows. **RANGE:** Uncommon Caribbean, Bahamas; not reported S. Florida.

NINELINED GOBY *Ginsburgellus novemlineatus*
SIZE: ½-¾ in., max. 1 in.
Gobies – Gobiidae
ID: Nine neon blue lines encircle body. Dark bluish brown to black with pale orangish to salmon head. Inhabit rocky limestone shorelines and tidepools. Take shelter under Rock-Boring Urchins, and occasionally Long Spined Urchins. **RANGE:** Rare Caribbean, Bahamas; not reported S. Florida.

TIGER GOBY *Tigrigobius macrodon*
SIZE: 1½-1¾ in., max. 2 in.
Gobies – Gobiidae
ID: Nearly transparent with dark, narrow rings encircling body and head. Clear fins. **RANGE:** Occasional S. Florida southward to central Caribbean; not reported Bahamas or southern Caribbean.

BLACKRINGED GOBY *Tigrigobius zebrellus*
SIZE: 1½-1¾ in., max. 2 in.
Gobies – Gobiidae
ID: Head and body encircled with black bars. Bright yellow from snout to dorsal fin, remainder of body bright blue. Fins clear. **RANGE:** Common Venezuela and Tinidad.

ORANGESIDED GOBY
Elacatinus dilepis
Gobies – Gobiidae
SIZE: ½-¾ in., max. 1 in.
ID: Two large, reddish orange squares outlined in black behind pectoral fin and below lateral line. Red and white dashes, separated by black, along lateral line. Red and black markings on head. Rear body translucent. Perch on the surface of sponges and coral heads. **RANGE:** Occasional to uncommon Caribbean, Bahamas; not reported S. Florida.

82

RUSTY GOBY
Priolepis hipoliti
Gobies – Gobiidae
SIZE: 1/2-1 in., max. 1 1/4 in.
ID: Orange spots on dorsal, tail and anal fins. Shades of brown to red-brown to orange; iris red to gold, pupil green. Second dorsal spine elongate. Perch upside down on ceilings of small recesses in reefs or under rocks. **RANGE:** Occasional Caribbean, Bahamas, S. Florida.

LEOPARD GOBY   *Tigrigobius saucrus*
SIZE: 1/2-3/4 in., max. 1 in.   Gobies – Gobiidae
ID: Rusty brown spots on body. Pale translucent to transparent background; occasionally have pinkish tints, especially on head; red to reddish brown spots and markings on head. White backbone usually visible. **RANGE:** Uncommon Caribbean, S. Florida; not reported Bahamas.

PEPPERMINT GOBY   *Coryphopterus lipernes*
SIZE: 1/2-1 in., max. 1 1/4 in.   Gobies – Gobiidae
ID: Electric blue wash on snout. Yellow-gold to translucent body. Several pale red to olive lines run from behind eye to forebody. Second spine of spinous dorsal fin of males noticeably long [pictured]. Perch on living corals. **RANGE:** Common to occasional Caribbean, Bahamas, S. Florida.

MASKED/GLASS GOBY
Coryphopterus personatus/hyalinus
Gobies – Gobiidae
SIZE: 3/4-1 1/4 in., max. 1 1/2 in.
ID: Series of small white rectangles on lateral line. Bright orange to translucent. Dark "mask" covers area between eyes and snout. Second spine of spinous dorsal fin of males is noticeably long [pictured]. (Note: There is no reliable way to visually distinguish between these two similar appearing species underwater — in hand examination of physical features is required.) Hover in small to large aggregations just inside or near recesses in the reef. **RANGE:** Abundant to common Caribbean, Bahamas, S. Florida.

ORANGESPOTTED GOBY
Nes longus
Gobies – Gobiidae
SIZE: 2-3 in., max. 4 in.
ID: Five to seven paired dark spots along midbody (often with dusky extensions that form bars). Noticeably elongate body. Shades of tan to light gray with numerous, often orangish, spots and small blotches; orangish spots on dorsal and tail fins tend to form bands. Adults have long first dorsal spine. Live in commensal relationship with blind snapping shrimp that build and maintain burrows in mud, silt and sand. Fish perch in front of burrow and warn shrimp of danger by fin movements, causing shrimp and fish to instantly retreat into burrow.
RANGE: Uncommon Caribbean, Bahamas, S. Florida.

CRESTED GOBY   *Lophogobius cyprinoides*
SIZE: 1-3 in., max. 4 in.   Gobies – Gobiidae
ID: Rounded, fleshy crest on top of head. Shades of brown to olive-brown or red-brown. Inhabit shallow, sheltered waters including bays, inlets, tidal creeks, canals and rocky areas near mangroves. **RANGE:** Common Caribbean, Bahamas, S. Florida.

FRILLFIN GOBY   *Bathygobius* spp.
SIZE: 1-4 in., max. 6 in.   Gobies – Gobiidae
ID: Bluntly rounded head with large mouth. Usually 5-6 wide, dusky to dark bars across back. Highly variable shades of drab brown to gray, often with speckles, spots and mottling. Inhabit tide pools and inshore areas of sand and seagrasses. **RANGE:** Occasional Caribbean, Bahamas, S. Florida.

SEMINOLE GOBY   *Microgobius carri*
SIZE: 1¼-2½ in., max. 3 in.   Gobies – Gobiidae
ID: Bright yellow body stripe continues onto tail. Pearly white; bluish tints often on back and yellow tints often on lower head. Hover just above burrows in the sand in depths from 20-70 ft. **RANGE:** Occasional to uncommon Caribbean, Bahamas, S. Florida.

BANNER GOBY   *Microgobius microlepis*
SIZE: 1-1½ in., max. 2 in.   Gobies – Gobiidae
ID: Bluish and orangish streaks on cheek. Lower dorsal fin light to dark red; yellow line on upper rear dorsal runs onto tail. Mated pairs inhabit burrows in fine sand. Females often swollen with eggs. **RANGE:** Occasional, but can be locally abundant northwest Caribbean, Bahamas, S. Florida.

HOVERING DARTFISH   *Ptereleotris helenae*
SIZE: 2-4 in., max. 5 in.   Dartfishes – Ptereleotridae
ID: Rounded tail. Bluish gray; fins often yellowish. May have faint yellow, red and blue markings. Hover above burrows in sand between 35 and 130 ft. **RANGE:** Occasional S. Florida, east and central Caribbean; rare western Caribbean, Bahamas.

Hovering Dartfish – Juvenile   **SIZE:** 1-3 in.
ID: Bluish with bright yellow tail. Juveniles more frequently encountered than adults. Can be solitary, but most commonly in groups numbering in the dozens.

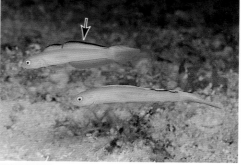

BLUESTRIPE DARTFISH   *Ptereleotris randalli*
SIZE: 2-3 in., max. 4 in.   Dartfishes – Ptereleotridae
ID: Bright blue to blue-green stripe runs from between eyes to foredorsal fin. Reddish cream to bluish gray with translucent fins. Hover above burrows in the sand, feeding on plankton. **RANGE:** Occasional coast of Venezuela to St. Vincent in the eastern Caribbean.

BLUE DARTFISH   *Ptereleotris calliura*
SIZE: 2-4 in., max. 5 in.   Dartfishes – Ptereleotridae
ID: Narrow black to red sub-marginal stripe on dorsal fin. Long, pointed tail. Hover just above burrows in the sand. Typically solitary, but occasionally in pairs. Dive into their burrow when disturbed. **RANGE:** Common to occasional S. Florida. Not reported Caribbean, Bahamas.

RINGED SHY BLENNY COMPLEX   *Starksia hassi* complex
SIZE: 1/2-1 1/4 in., max. 1 3/4 in.   Scaly Blennies – Labrisomidae
ID: There are seven complexes within the genus *Starksia* with 21 or more species. This one has shades of brown with pale rings on the body. **RANGE:** Uncommon to rare Caribbean, Bahamas, S. Florida.

EELGRASS BLENNY   *Stathmonotus stahli*
SIZE: 3/4-1 1/4 in., max. 1 1/2 in.   Tube Blennies – Chaenopsidae
ID: Green body (uncommonly brown). Elongate body scales; rounded tail. Spines the entire length of dorsal and anal fins; paddle-like cirrus above each eye. Inhabit sea grassbeds and adjoing rubble. **RANGE:** Occasional to uncommon Florida, Bahamas, Caribbean.

Blennies

HAIRY BLENNY COMPLEX *Labrisomus* spp.
SIZE: 2¹/₂ -6 in., max. 9 in.   Scaly Blennies – Labrisomidae
ID: This complex has three members. **Most have dark spot on upper gill cover.** Bluntish head with thick lips and large eyes. Yellow-brown to brown, red-brown to nearly black. Hide in shallow inshore rocky areas and rubble. **RANGE:** Occasional Caribbean, Bahamas, S. Florida.

Hairy Blenny Complex
ID: Body markings vary from distinctive banding to heavy spotting. Courting males have bright red or orange heads.

PUFFCHEECK BLENNY *Gobioclinus bucciferus*
SIZE: 2-3 in., max. 3¹/₂ in.   Scaly Blennies – Labrisomidae
ID: Wide dark band below, and two spots or lines behind large "goggle" eyes with yellowish iris. Four or five irregular bars become somewhat wider at midbody and continue onto belly. Inhabit shallow areas of sand and rubble. **RANGE:** Uncommon Caribbean, Bahamas, S. Florida.

PALEHEAD BLENNY *Gobioclinus gobio*
SIZE: 1¹/₂ -2¹/₄ in., max. 2¹/₂ in   Scaly Blennies – Labrisomidae
ID: Iris of large "goggle" eyes white with numerous fine-line markings and black spot behind eye. Four or five irregular body bars become wider and darker at midbody. Prefer shallow rocky areas, but also inhabit deeper reefs. **RANGE:** Uncommon Caribbean, Bahamas, S. Florida.

DOWNY BLENNY *Gobioclinus kalisherae*
SIZE: 2-3 in., max. 3¹/₂ in.   Scaly Blennies – Labrisomidae
ID: Four or five indistinct bars of even pigmentation. Blunt head with thick lips and large "goggle" eyes. Shades of red-brown to greenish brown. Numerous spots on fin rays, especially pectorals. **RANGE:** Uncommon continental coasts of Caribbean, S. Florida; not reported Bahamas, Caribbean islands.

SPOTCHEEK BLENNY *Brockius nigricinctus*
SIZE: 1¹/₄-2¹/₂ in., max. 3 in.   Scaly Blennies – Labrisomidae
ID: Large, dark ocellated spot on gill cover. Eight or nine body bars extend from dorsal fin to belly. Most common in shallows where they seek refuge under rocks, rubble and sea urchins. **RANGE:** Rare Caribbean, Bahamas, S. Florida.

QUILLFIN BLENNY   *Brockius filamentosus*
SIZE: 2-4 in., max. 5 in.   Scaly Blennies – Labrisomidae
ID: Elongate foredorsal fin (male more elongate, with two or three distinct points and yellow highlights). Ocellated dark spot behind gill covers of males and females. Dark tan to reddish brown. Dark brown body bars. **RANGE:** Uncommon to rare Caribbean and southern Bahamas, not reported S. Florida.

Quillfin Blenny – Female
ID: Black and gray mottled dorsal, tail and pectoral fins.

DIAMOND BLENNY   *Malacoctenus boehlkei*
SIZE: 1½-2¼ in., max. 2½ in. Scaly Blennies – Labrisomidae
ID: Dark (black to dark blue) ocellated spot near front of dorsal fin. Pale gray to tan; head most commonly bright yellow to gold, occasionally brown; may have red spots on head and body. Dorsal fin transparent behind area of ocellated spot. **RANGE:** Occasional Caribbean, Bahamas, not reported S. Florida.

Diamond Blenny – Variation
ID: Seem to have regional color variations, and in some areas associate with Giant Anemones.

MARBLED BLENNY   *Paraclinus marmoratus*
SIZE: 2-3 in., max. 4 in.   Scaly Blennies – Labrisomidae
ID: Two (occasionally three) large yellowish green ocellated spots on rear dorsal fin. First two spines of foredorsal fin elongate. Tan to dark brown; often display pale spots and marbling. Large noticeable scales. Inhabit seagrass and shallow reefs. **RANGE:** Uncommon Caribbean, Bahamas, S. Florida.

BANDED BLENNY   *Paraclinus fasciatus*
SIZE: 1¼-1¾ in., max. 2¼ in. Scaly Blennies – Labrisomidae
ID: Dark bar across base of tail. Pair of paddlelike cirri usually with three small points, far back on nape near dorsal fin. Light to dark brown and gray; often display pattern of dusky to dark body bars. Large noticeable scales. **RANGE:** Uncommon Caribbean, Bahamas, S. Florida.

Blennies

SADDLED BLENNY *Malacoctenus triangulatus*
SIZE: 1¹/₂ -2¹/₄ in., max. 2¹/₂ in. Scaly Blennies – Labrisomidae
ID: Four dark, inverted, triangular markings form "saddles" across back. Undercolor white or occasionally yellow to orange. Faint, diamond-shaped patterns often on lower body. Bar at base of tail. **RANGE:** Common to occasional Caribbean, Bahamas, S. Florida.

Saddled Blenny – Variation
ID: Occasionally display red dots on body prominently concentrated in dark areas.

DUSKY BLENNY *Malacoctenus gilli*
SIZE: 1¹/₂ -2¹/₂ in., max. 3 in. Scaly Blennies – Labrisomidae
ID: Large ocellated spot toward rear overlaps dorsal fin and body. Gray, greenish or reddish tints; alternating light and dusky body bars; banding on lower head. Inhabit shallow rubble in surge to 15 ft. **RANGE:** Occasional S. Caribbean; uncommon remainder of Caribbean, Bahamas; not reported S. Florida.

GOLDLINE BLENNY *Malacoctenus aurolineatus*
SIZE: 1-2 in., max. 2¹/₂ in. Scaly Blennies – Labrisomidae
ID: Three dark bars on forebody, the second and third are joined near the center forming an H-shape. Rear half of body yellowish with two to four darkish, often indistinct bars. Line markings on underside of head. Shallow depths to 20 ft. **RANGE:** Occasional Caribbean, Bahamas, S. Florida.

BARFIN BLENNY *Malacoctenus versicolor*
SIZE: 1¹/₂ -2 in., max. 2¹/₂ in. Scaly Blennies – Labrisomidae
ID: Dark, wide bars extend from dorsal fin to belly widening at midbody. Pair of bushy cirri above eyes and another pair on nape. Undercolor brown to greenish brown, often some red on dorsal fins, pale toward belly. **RANGE:** Occasional to rare Caribbean, Bahamas; Uncommon S. Florida.

Barfin Blenny – Female
ID: Light yellow-brown undercolor with darker yellow-brown to brown bars similar to males. Note cirri above eyes and on nape.

ROSY BLENNY *Malacoctenus macropus*
SIZE: 1½-2 in., max. 2¼ in.   Scaly Blennies – Labrisomidae
ID: Sharply pointed snout. MALE: Red spots and markings on underside of head and cheeks. Vary, from wide dark bars on back becoming lighter at midline to almost black. **RANGE:** Common to occasional S. Florida; occasional Caribbean, Bahamas.

Rosy Blenny – Female
ID: No red spots or dependable markings. Vary, from a few dark spots on back to wide, often indistinct, dark bars on back that lighten dramatically near midline, often disappearing completely.

SEAWEED BLENNY *Parablennius marmoreus*
SIZE: 1½-3 in., max. 3½ in.   Combtooth Blennies – Blenniidae
ID: Highly variable colors and markings. **Pale blue vertical line markings (occasionally netlike) down snout, over upper lip and below eyes.** Series of dark spots often form broken stripes on body; stripe from eye to tail usually widest and darkest. **RANGE:** Common to occasional Caribbean, Bahamas, Florida.

Seaweed Blenny – Variation
ID: Usually in shades of earthtones, but can be solid bright yellow to gold. (Note diagnostic blue line markings on side of head.)

Seaweed Blenny – Variation
ID: Can pale or darken and change markings to blend with background. Blunt snout. Cirri above eyes usually have three or four branches.

Seaweed Blenny – Variation
ID: Often mottled in shades of brown on whitish background.

Blennies

REDLIP BLENNY *Ophioblennius macclurei*
SIZE: 2½-4½ in., max. 5 in.   Combtooth Blennies – Blenniidae
ID: Blunt, reddish brown head; large size; often with reddish lips. Pectoral fins and upper border of tail may be edged and tinted with yellow to gold or red. Perch on reef crests and rocks in shallow water from 5-25 ft. **RANGE:** Common to occasional Caribbean, Bahamas, S. Florida.

Redlip Blenny – Variation
ID: Vary from dark reddish brown to bicolor with gray or nearly all gray (most commonly bicolored).

MOLLY MILLER *Scartella cristata*
SIZE: 1½- 3 in., max. 4 in.   Combtooth Blennies – Blenniidae
ID: Fringe of brushlike cirri (usually red and white banded) on top of head. Shades of olive-brown, can be quite pale or very dark. Variable dark markings, occasionally with white spots; tail usually banded. Inhabit rocky shallows with surge. **RANGE:** Occasional to rare Caribbean, Bahamas, S. Florida.

PEARL BLENNY *Entomacrodus nigricans*
SIZE: 2-3 in., max. 4 in.   Combtooth Blennies – Blenniidae
ID: Paired dark blotches on side. Shades of brownish green with numerous dark speckles and spots on head and foreback. Scattering of bluish white to pearly white spots. Inhabit shallow rocky coasts with surf and swells. **RANGE:** Uncommon Caribbean, Bahamas, S. Florida.

LONGHORN BLENNY *Hypsoblennius exstochilus*
SIZE: 1-2 in., max. 2¼ in.   Combtooth Blennies – Blenniidae
ID: Extremely tall cirri above eye with numerous secondary branches. Yellow head; pale yellow-gold body; fins have yellowish cast. Dark golden to brown bar extends from cirri, across eye and cheek. **RANGE:** Uncommon Bahamas; rare Caribbean; not reported S. Florida.

TESSELLATED BLENNY *Hypsoblennius invemar*
SIZE: 1-2 in., max. 2½ in.   Combtooth Blennies – Blenniidae
ID: Head and body covered with brilliant orange spots or polygons outlined in black. Dark blue. Adults may have up to four branches on cirri above eyes. Inhabit barnacle shells in shallow water; most common on pilings. **RANGE:** Uncommon Caribbean, S. Florida; not reported Bahamas.

WRASSE BLENNY *Hemiemblemaria simula*
SIZE: 2-3^1/$_2$ in., max. 4 in.   Tube Blennies – Chaenopsidae
ID: Mimic yellow phases of Bluehead (cleaner wrasse). **Black dot on foredorsal fin does not extend onto body.** Corners of mouth extend to below eyes. Often sit in holes, with their heads protruding. **RANGE:** Occasional Bahamas, S. Florida to Central America; not reported Caribbean islands.

Wrasse Blenny – Juvenile SIZE: 1-1^1/$_2$ in.
ID: Young have transparent fins and somewhat translucent body. A dark stripe runs from snout across eye to tail and has a teardrop-shaped end. Often hover under reef ledges mixed with other small fishes.

ARROW BLENNY *Lucayablennius zingaro*
SIZE: 1-1^1/$_2$ in., max. 2 in.   Tube Blennies – Chaenopsidae
ID: Long, pointed mouth and snout. Drift with tail "cocked." Reddish with several black blotches on dorsal and anal fins near tail. Unlike other blennies, rarely rest on fins; usually drift in secluded areas. **RANGE:** Occasional Caribbean, Bahamas; not reported S. Florida.

CALDWELL'S CARIBBEAN BLENNY *Emblemaria caldwelli*
SIZE: ^{3}/$_4$-1 in., max.1 ^{1}/$_2$ in.   Tube Blennies – Chaenopsidae
ID: Tall black foredorsal fin with a few scattered white spots. Long unbranched orbital cirri. Head and forebody shades of reddish brown with numerous small black spots. **RANGE:** Uncommon to rare Bahamas to Turks & Caicos Islands, Jamaica and Belize.

RED BANNER BLENNY *Emblemariopsis ramirezi*
SIZE: 1-1^1/$_4$ in., max. 2 in.   Tube Blennies – Chaenopsidae
ID: COURTING MALE – Inhabit small holes **turning black and raising red and white upper foredorsal fin.** At other times have brownish translucent bodies and inhabit shallow recesses. **RANGE:** Occasional coast of South America and Lesser Antilles to St. Vincent; not reported balance of Caribbean.

Red Banner Blenny – Female
ID: Reddish brown head with dark speckles; translucent body; tall white and black banded first dorsal spine. Dark bar on base of pectoral fin.

Blennies

SAILFIN BLENNY
Emblemaria pandionis
Tube Blennies – Chaenopsidae
SIZE: 1½ -2 in., max. 2½ in.
ID: COURTING MALE – Dark brown to black with extremely tall foredorsal fin only displayed when attracting mates or intimidating rival males. Typically mottled tan to brown to blend with bottom. Become reproductively active mid to late afternoon when females move about. When excited turn black and repeatedly extend dorsal fin, occasionally sailing an inch or two out of hole.
RANGE: Occasional Caribbean, S. Florida; uncommon Bahamas.

Sailfin Blenny – Male
ID: Spend much of day inhabiting shelter holes in bottom or pieces of rubble with head protruding. Depths from 3-35 ft. Change from typical mottled brown color to black when attracting mates or defending shelter holes from rival males. Form small to large clusters that can number in the dozens. Can be difficult to find when not reproductively active.

Sailfin Blenny – Female
ID: Pale and mottled in shades of brown to gray with tall dorsal fin (not as large as those of males). Remain in shelter holes with head protruding much of day; commonly move freely about blending with bottom in mid to late afternoon when reproductively active.

SPINY SAILFIN BLENNY   *Emblemaria diphyodontis*
SIZE: 1½ - 2¼ in., max. 2½ in. Tube Blennies – Chaenopsidae
ID: MALE – U-shaped notches in soft tissue connecting first, second and third spines of tall foredorsal fin. Lighter color to match background when in holes with head protruding; turn dark when reproductively active. **RANGE:** Common Venezuela including inshore islands; uncommon Grenadines.

RIBBON BLENNY   *Emblemaria vitta*
SIZE: 1-1½ in., max. 2 in.   Tube Blennies – Chaenopsidae
ID: MALE – Yellow to orange blotch on base of extremely tall foredorsal fin. Tan to dark forebody, translucent toward rear. Sit in shelter holes in sand and rubble bottoms with only head protruding. **RANGE:** Rare central Caribbean, Bahamas, S. Florida.

YELLOWFACE PIKEBLENNY
Chaenopsis limbaughi
Tube Blennies – Chaenopsidae
SIZE: 2-3 in., max. 3½ in.

ID: Soda straw thin eel-like body with pointed snout. Can only be identified from similar-appearing Bluethroat Pikeblenny [below] when large dorsal spine is raised showing **a black spot between first two spines encircled by a white ring,** often with a small orange area above. Occasionally additional spots on dorsal fin and yellow throat. Typically inhabit shallow sand, rubble and grassy areas where they often occupy abandoned worm tubes. **RANGE:** Uncommon Caribbean, Bahamas, S. Florida.

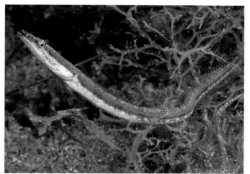

Yellowface Pikeblenny – Female
ID: Shades of brown to greenish brown to gray, often with pale speckles and dark midbody stripe. Positive identification can only be made by noting interaction with identified male.

Bluethroat Pikeblenny – Female
ID: Shades of brown to gray, often with pale speckles and dark midbody stripe. Positive identification can only be made by noting interaction with identified male.

BLUETHROAT PIKEBLENNY
Chaenopsis ocellata
Tube Blennies – Chaenopsidae
SIZE: 3-4 in., max. 5 in.

ID: Soda straw thin eel-like body with pointed snout. **Curved black mark between first two spines with white rear edge, often with adjacent orange patch.** Typically inhabit shallow sand, rubble and grassy areas where they often occupy abandoned worm tubes. **RANGE:** Occasional S. Florida; rare Bahamas, Greater Antilles.

SECRETARY BLENNY
Acanthemblemaria maria
Tube Blennies – Chaenopsidae
SIZE: ³/₄ -1¹/₂ in., max. 2 in.
ID: Whitish streak behind and below eye. Dark black to brown head and body with white speckles, occasionally mottled. Branched cirri above eye. Several irregular brown and pale body bars. Large, dark spot (often navy blue) behind eye, but may not be apparent when head is a solid dark color. Reddish to yellow patch of tall spines on nape. Most commonly inhabit small worm holes in white limestone rocks where they perch with heads extended occasionally darting out to grab microscopic particles of drifting food. **RANGE:** Common Caribbean; uncommon to rare Bahamas; rare S. Florida.

ROUGHHEAD BLENNY *Acanthemblemaria aspera*
SIZE: ³/₄ -1¹/₄ in., max. 1¹/₂ in. Tube Blennies – Chaenopsidae
ID: Densely branched, bushy cirri above eye. Numerous short spines on top of head form a rear pointing "V". Vary from black to brown, tan, olive, yellow and white; often lighter toward rear of body. Brown and white speckles on head and body. **RANGE:** Common S. Florida; uncommon Caribbean, Bahamas.

Roughhead Blenny – Male
ID: MALE – Ocellated black spot on foredorsal fin; courting males have dark heads and forebodies. **FEMALE –** May have dark smudge on foredorsal fin, but never an ocellated spot, usually lighter in color, some nearly white. Most commonly inhabit small worm holes in white limestone rocks with heads extended; dart out to grab suspended particles of food.

SPINYHEAD BLENNY
Acanthemblemaria spinosa
Tube Blennies – Chaenopsidae
SIZE: ³/₄ -1 in., max. 1¹/₄ in.
ID: Numerous short spines on top of head. Cirri above eye often have only two branches, and never more than a few, toward tip. Vary from black to brown, tan, and olive. Yellow-green "goggle" eyes. Dark black to brown head and body with white speckles, and occasionally mottled or with indistinct bands. Snout and nape usually white or greenish. Most commonly inhabit small worm holes in white limestone rocks where they perch with heads extended occasionally darting out to grab microscopic particles of drifting food. **RANGE:** Common Caribbean; occasional S.E. Florida; uncommon Bahamas. .

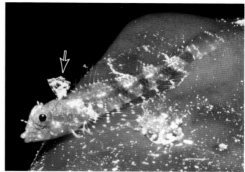

MEDUSA BLENNY *Acanthemblemaria medusa*
SIZE: $^3/_4$-1$^1/_4$ in., max. 1$^1/_2$ in.   Tube Blennies – Chaenopsidae
ID: **Bushy, highly branched cirri above eyes and long, pointed unbranched papillae on nape.** Large brown and black blotches and dark speckling on eyes and body. **RANGE:** Occasional to uncommon Lesser Antilles to Venezuela and Bonaire.

BLACKEDGE TRIPLEFIN *Enneanectes atrorus*
SIZE: 1-1$^1/_4$ in., max. 1$^1/_2$ in. Triplefin Blennies – Tripterygiidae
ID: **Long pointy snout with tall, usually white first dorsal fin.** Pale orange to reddish head and body with five dark, similar width, usually somewhat diagonal, bars on body. **RANGE:** Common to Occasional Florida, Bahamas, Caribbean.

ROUGHHEAD TRIPLEFIN *Enneanectes boehlkei*
SIZE: 1-1$^1/_4$ in., max. 1$^1/_2$ in. Triplefin Blennies – Tripterygiidae
ID: **Dark to black band on tail base proceeded by a narrower, white area.** Blunt snout; body usually shades of brown with four darkish bars. **RANGE:** Occasional to uncommon Florida, Bahamas, Caribbean.

LOFTY TRIPLEFIN *Enneanectes altivelis*
SIZE: 1-1$^1/_4$ in., max. 1$^1/_2$ in. Triplefin Blennies – Tripterygiidae
ID: **Tall first dorsal fin with three spines.** Head orangish brown; body pale translucent to brown; three or four dusky, often somewhat indistinct, body bars appear diagonal and may fork below midline. **RANGE:** Occasional to rare S. Florida, Bahamas, Caribbean.

LANCER DRAGONET *Paradiplogrammus bairdi*
SIZE: 1-2$^1/_2$ in., max. 4$^1/_2$ in.   Dragonets – Callionymidae
ID: **Large "goggle" eyes extend above flattened head.** First dorsal fin elongate; yellowish in males, blackish in females. Body mottled and marbled in shades ranging from pale whitish gray to brown and reddish brown. Can pale or darken. **RANGE:** Occasional Caribbean, Bahamas, S. Florida.

Lancer Dragonet – Female SIZE: $^3/_4$-1$^1/_2$ in.
ID: Females smaller than males and have a shorter black foredorsal fin. Inhabit areas of mixed coral rubble and sand often adjacent to reefs. Actively feed on bottom during the day blending into background. Tend to be solitary, but form loose group late each afternoon when reproductively active.

95

Jawfishes

YELLOWHEAD JAWFISH *Opistognathus aurifrons*
SIZE: 2-3 in., max. 4 in.   Jawfishes – Opistognathidae
ID: Yellowish head and pale body. Hover vertically above burrows in sand areas near reefs. Head varies from bright yellow to yellowish tan; body ranges from tan to bluish pearl; rear dorsal, anal and tail fins have bluish cast. Form small colonies. **RANGE:** Common Caribbean, Bahamas, S. Florida.

Yellowhead Jawfish – Variation
ID: Marked with blue bar behind eye and dark spot above upper rear eye. This variation is known from the southeastern Caribbean, St. Vincent to Tobago.

BANDED JAWFISH *Opistognathus macrognathus*
SIZE: 4-6½ in., max. 8 in.   Jawfishes – Opistognathidae
ID: Several blotches along sides. Blotch on outer half of dorsal fin starting behind sixth spine. Light tan head with indistinct, unpatterned markings. Inhabit rock-lined burrows in areas of coral rubble, rocks and sand. **RANGE:** Uncommon Caribbean, Bahamas, S. Florida.

DUSKY JAWFISH *Opistognathus whitehursti*
SIZE: 2½-3½ in., max. 4 in.   Jawfishes – Opistognathidae
ID: Blue to bluish black spot between second and fourth or fifth dorsal spines. Rear gill cover rounded. Mottled in shades of brown. Dorsal fin often has black edge, especially in larger individuals. **RANGE:** Uncommon Caribbean, Bahamas, S. Florida.

YELLOW JAWFISH *Opistognathus gilberti*
SIZE: 1½-2½ in., max. 3 in.   Jawfishes – Opistognathidae
ID: MALE – Black spot on foredorsal fin. White dorsal, anal and ventral fins. Head and body highly variable from yellowish silver to yellow also gray, powder blue and lavender. **RANGE:** Uncommon to rare Bahamas, western Caribbean, Jamaica and Puerto Rico; not reported S. Florida and balance of Caribbean.

Yellow Jawfish – Juvenile   SIZE: 1½-2½ in.
ID: Yellow to yellowish median stripe in dorsal and anal fins. Inhabit burrows in deep areas of sand, silt, calcareous rubble and coralline algae from 80-180 ft.

Odd-Shaped Bottom-Dwellers
Flounders – Scorpionfishes – Frogfishes
Pipefishes & Seahorses – Others

This ID Group consists of fishes that normally rest on the bottom and do not have a typical fishlike shape. All are experts at camouflage.

| Flounders
6 species, pg. 98 | Scorpionfishes
5 species, pg.102 | Frogfishes
6 species, pg. 106 | Pipefishes & Seahorses
7 species, pg. 108 |

Flounders, Bothidae – Flounders are unique, flat fishes that actually lie on their sides, not their bellies. While in their pelagic stage larval flounders have typical bilateral fish-shaped bodies, properly aligned fins and one eye on each side of their heads. Just before settling to the shallow seafloor, muscles, skin, blood vessels and bones slowly shift into the flattened shape of a benthic juvenile with both eyes on the upper side of their bodies. The eyes protrude noticeably, sometimes appearing to be raised on short stalks. Their exposed pectoral fin appears more like a dorsal fin, while the dorsal and anal fins ring the rounded body. Flounders can change colors and lighten or darken to blend with the bottom. Many enhance their camouflage by partly burying themselves. When on the move, they glide over the bottom in a wavelike motion. Many flounders appear similar, but can be identified to species with careful attention to subtle markings.

Scorpionfishes, Scorpaenidae – Fleshy appendages, or flaps, help camouflage these lie-in-wait predators' large heads and stocky bodies. Mottled and spotted in earthtones, they are difficult to detect as they rest on bottom rubble and/or algae. Spines of the first dorsal fin, which can be raised for defense, are venomous and can inflict a painful wound. Their pectoral fins are often brightly colored, but unseen unless spread. Although species are quite similar at first glance, most can easily be distinguished with attention to detail.

Frogfishes, Antennariidae – Frogfishes are globular with large, extremely upturned mouths, which can open in a split second to the width of their bodies to suck in prey. Their pectoral and ventral fins have evolved into webbed, handlike appendages used to grasp, perch, or "walk". Small, circular gill openings are located behind the pectoral fins. The first dorsal spine, located on the snout, has evolved into a thin rod with a fleshy bait attached to the end, which is jigged in front of their mouths to attract prey. Masters at camouflage, most species can, over a period of day or weeks, change their color to match new backgrounds. At rest they often look like sponges or clumps of algae. Body markings are used as keys for identification.

Pipefishes & Seahorses, Syngnathidae – These strange little fishes have trumpetlike snouts and small mouths used to suck in prey. Their bodies are encased in protective bony rings. Seahorses are vertically oriented, and have a cocked head. Their finless, elongated tail base is often coiled around a hold-fast to maintain position. Pipefishes are elongated, snakelike bottom-dwellers with heads extending straight from their bodies, and small tail fins.

Flounders – Soles – Tonguefishes

PEACOCK FLOUNDER
Bothus lunatus

Lefteye Flounders – Bothidae

SIZE: 6-15 in., max. 18 in.

ID: Numerous blue rosettes over entire body. Shades of brown to tan. Can darken or pale and change color dramatically. Notch in upper head profile above lips. Numerous blue spots on fins and head. Inhabit sand, coral rubble and seagrass, often near patch reefs. Often rest motionless on bottom, relying on camouflage. Glide over bottom with wavelike motion. Males display brightest colors and raise elongate pectoral fin on upper body during courtship or competition with other males. **RANGE:** Common Caribbean, Bahamas, S. Florida.

Peacock Flounder – Female   **SIZE:** 6-10 in.
ID: Smaller size and pectoral fin on upper body much shorter than males.

Peacock Flounder – Variation
ID: Master of camouflage, can instantly alter colors and body markings to match surroundings.

MACULATED FLOUNDER   *Bothus maculiferus*
SIZE: 5-8 in., max. 10 in.   Lefteye Flounders – Bothidae
ID: Male [on right] has three long, separate pectoral fin rays. Scattering of pale blue to gold rings and spots over body, fins and head. Shades of brown to tan and pale grayish white. **RANGE:** Occasional to rare Caribbean, Bahamas; not reported S. Florida.

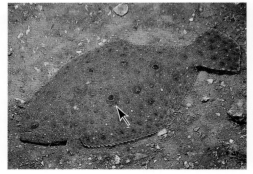

GULF FLOUNDER   *Paralichthys albigutta*
SIZE: 6-10 in., max. 15 in.   Sand Flounder – Bothidae
ID: Three large ocellated spots with dark centers form a rear-pointing triangular pattern on back (often have several additional similar, but smaller spots). Tan to gray. **RANGE:** Common to occasional Florida and Gulf of Mexico to Panama.

EYED FLOUNDER
Bothus ocellatus

Lefteye Flounders – Bothidae

SIZE: 4-5½ in., max. 7 in.

ID: Body covered with brown to tan rosettes and spots. Small nearly circular body. Shades of brown to tan. Can darken or pale and change color dramatically to match bottom. Have dark, diffuse area near center of lateral line. Widely spaced eyes set on diagonal. Two dark, sometimes faint, tail spots near the base, one above the other. Inhabit sand, coral rubble and seagrass areas, often near patch reefs. Rest motionless on bottom, blending with background. When moving, glide over bottom with wavelike motion.

RANGE: Occasional Caribbean, Bahamas, S. Florida.

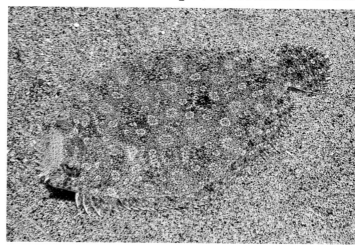

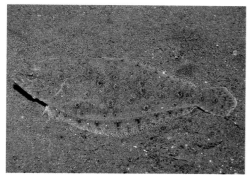

CHANNEL FLOUNDER
Syacium micrurum

SIZE: 4-9 in., max. 1 ft.   Sand Flounders – Paralichthyidae

ID: Body covered with brown to tan rosettes and spots. Shades of brown to tan. Eyes close-set; several dark spots along lateral line. Widely spaced, dark vertical lines on dorsal and anal fins. **RANGE:** Occasional Caribbean, Bahamas, S. Florida.

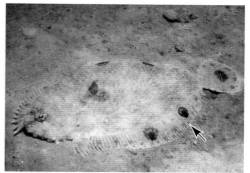

SPOTFIN FLOUNDER
Cyclopsetta fimbriata

SIZE: 5-10 in., max. 13 in.   Sand Flounders – Paralichthyidae

ID: Two large ocellated spots on both the dorsal and anal fins, and single spot on center of tail. Change color in shades of brown to gray. Three or four obscure spots on tail margin. Dusky to dark blotch on outer half of pectoral fin. **RANGE:** Occasional Caribbean, Bahamas, S. Florida.

HOGCHOKER
Trinectes maculates

SIZE: 2-5 in., max. 8 in.   American Soles – Achiridae

ID: Zebra-striped pattern of 7-8 bars on body. Medium brown to brownish gray or nearly black. **RANGE:** Uncommon Florida, western Caribbean and northern South America to Tobago.

SPOTTEDFIN TONGUEFISH
Symphurus diomedeanus

SIZE: 1-3 in.   Tonguefishes – Cynoglossidae

ID: JUVENILE – Several large spots on rear dorsal and anal fins. Shades of brown with some obscure mottling. Juv. inhabit shallow grass beds. Rest on and blend with bottom. Adults inhabit depths below 150 feet. **RANGE:** Rare S. Florida and continental coast, including inshore islands to Venezuela.

Clingfishes – Batfishes – Toadfishes

RED CLINGFISH *Acyrtus rubiginosus*

SIZE: ³/₄-1¹/₄ in., max. 1¹/₂ in. Clingfishes – Gobiesocidae

ID: Two white bands extend from lower eye across cheek. Red-brown; occasionally has narrow red bands across rear head and body. Wide, flat rounded head. **RANGE:** Uncommon Caribbean, Bahamas; not reported S. Florida.

STIPPLED CLINGFISH *Gobiesox punctulatus*

SIZE: 1-2 in., max. 2¹/₂ in. Clingfishes – Gobiesocidae

ID: Numerous, scattered, tiny black spots on upper side, especially on head. Pale tan to brown, or olive. Occasionally have bands across body behind head. Wide, flat, rounded head. Often attach to underside of ledges and rocks. **RANGE:** Uncommon Caribbean, Bahamas; not reported S. Florida.

SHORTNOSE BATFISH

Ogcocephalus nasutus

Batfishes – Ogcocephalidae

SIZE: 6-12 in., max. 15 in.

ID: Two dark bands border pale band on tail. Unicornlike projection between eye quite variable in length and usually with tuft on tip. Mottled reddish brown to tan. Variable markings from nearly uniform color to many dark spots outlined in white or with numerous white line markings, occasionally some yellowish areas on back. Older individuals have the shortest projections. **RANGE:** Uncommon Caribbean, Bahamas, S. Florida.

Shortnose Batfish – Variation

ID: Rare red with white blotches. Note short projection between eye indicating an older individual.

Shortnose Batfish – Variation

ID: Generally take on the coloring of their background for camouflage.

ROUGHBACK BATFISH *Ogcocephalus parvus*
SIZE: 2-3 in., max. 4 in. Batfishes – Ogcocephalidae
ID: Pectoral fins light red to reddish brown, or white with wide black band at tip. Tail fin pale to white with wide, dark margin. Mottled shades of olive to yellowish brown or reddish brown. Numerous fleshy tabs and threadlike projections usually on back. **RANGE:** Rare Caribbean, S. Florida.

PANCAKE BATFISH *Halieutichthys aculeatus*
SIZE: 2-3½ in., max. 4 in. Batfishes – Ogcocephalidae
ID: Flat head, and forebody rounded like a "pancake." Vary from reddish or yellowish brown to tan, olive or gray; may have bright yellow pectoral fins. Short projection between eyes. **RANGE:** Rare Caribbean, Bahamas, S. Florida.

SPLENDID TOADFISH *Sanopus splendidus*
SIZE: 4-6 in., max. 8 in. Toadfishes – Batrachoididae
ID: Zebra-striped head. Mottled and patched in shades of brown, magenta and gray over white. Well-developed head and unbranched chin barbels. Margins of fins yellow except ventrals, which are solid yellow. Flattened head, fanlike pectorals; rounded tail. **RANGE:** Common Cozumel; apparently endemic.

WHITELINED TOADFISH *Sanopus greenfieldorum*
SIZE: 4-10 in., max. 1 ft. Toadfishes – Batrachoididae
ID: Bright white lines cross head and radiate from eyes. Well-developed unbranched barbels on head and chin. Flattened head, fanlike pectoral fins and rounded tail. **RANGE:** Uncommon Belize; not reported elsewhere.

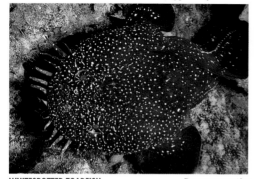

WHITESPOTTED TOADFISH *Sanopus astrifer*
SIZE: 4-10 in., max. 1 ft. Toadfishes – Batrachoididae
ID: Bright white spots cover dark body. Shades of dark brown; fins generally darker and often have bluish cast. Well-developed unbranched fleshy tabs on head and chin. Flattened head, fanlike pectoral fins and rounded tail. **RANGE:** Occasional to rare Belize; not reported elsewhere.

BEARDED TOADFISH *Sanopus barbatus*
SIZE: 6-8 in., max. 16 in. Toadfishes – Batrachoididae
ID: Projecting lower jaw with long pointed chin barbells with numerous branched side branches. Brown with some mottling. Flattened head, fanlike pectorals and rounded tail. **RANGE:** Uncommon Caribbean coast of Central America.

Scorpionfishes

COMMON LIONFISH
Pterois volitans
Scorpionfish – Scorpaenidae
SIZE: 6-15 in., max 17 in.

ID: Numerous reddish brown to nearly black bands with white lines between; **long featherlike pectoral fin rays with light and dark bands,** dark spotted dorsal, anal and tail fins. Solitary or in loose aggregations. Coastal, lagoon and seaward reefs. Hover just above bottom often under ledges. Native to the Indo-Pacific but has become an invasive species in much of the Tropical Western Atlantic. Venomous dorsal, ventral and anal fin spines. Similar-appearing *P. miles* has also invaded the Western Atlantic, but is rare. **RANGE:** Common to occasional much of Caribbean, Bahamas, S. Florida.

Common Lionfish – Intermediate   **SIZE:** 6-9 in.
ID: Body banding varies from light tan to reddish brown or black. Tend to remain near the bottom.

Common Lionfish – Juvenile   **SIZE:** 1½ -5 in.
ID: Long whitish pectoral fin spines and translucent tail.

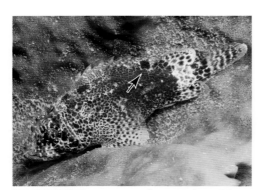

REEF SCORPIONFISH   *Scorpaenodes caribbaeus*
SIZE: 2-4 in., max. 5 in.   Scorpionfishes – Scorpaenidae
ID: Spotted pectoral, rear dorsal, anal and tail fins. Mottled dark brown to red-brown. May have white forebody and spinous dorsal fin. Dusky or dark spot on rear spinous dorsal fin. Nocturnal. **RANGE:** Occasional Caribbean, Bahamas, S. Florida.

PLUMED SCORPIONFISH   *Scorpaena grandicornis*
SIZE: 3½-5½ in., max. 7 in.   Scorpionfishes – Scorpaenidae
ID: Long, large, fleshy appendage (cirrus) or "plume" above each eye. Shades of mottled brown. Three dark bands on tail. Numerous skin flaps on body. **RANGE:** Occasional Florida; uncommon Caribbean; rare Bahamas.

SPOTTED SCORPIONFISH
Scorpaena plumieri
Scorpionfishes – Scorpaenidae
SIZE: 7-14 in., max. 18 in.
ID: Three dark bars on tail. Mottled, in wide range of browns and reds. Dusky band on rear body. Large skin flaps (plumes) above eyes may be absent. Often have numerous fleshy tabs on chin and head. Back side of pectoral fin, near base, has black area with brilliant white spots. **RANGE:** Common to occasional Caribbean, Bahamas, S. Florida.

Spotted Scorpionfish – Variation
ID: Lie-in-wait predators that rely on camouflage colors and growth of fleshy tabs to disguise their presence. Seldom move unless provoked.

Spotted Scorpionfish
ID: Occasionally move for short distances. Skim over the bottom with large pectoral fins extended to the side exposing white spots, origin of the species common name.

MUSHROOM SCORPIONFISH   *Scorpaena inermis*
SIZE: 1½-2½ in., max. 3 in.   Scorpionfishes – Scorpaenidae
ID: Fleshy, upside-down mushroom-shaped growths extend over upper eye (not always present). Dark margins on pectoral, soft dorsal, anal and tail fins. Two faint, thin bars midtail. **RANGE:** Common to occasional Caribbean; occasional to uncommon Bahamas, S. Florida.

BARBFISH   *Scorpaena brasiliensis*
SIZE: 6-10 in., max. 14 in.   Scorpionfishes – Scorpaenidae
ID: Two bars on tail at center and rear margin; black spot above pectoral fin and often one or more behind. Red to reddish brown or yellow to yellow brown. **RANGE:** Occasional Florida and continental coast to Brazil.

FLYING GURNARD *Dactylopterus volitans*
SIZE: 6-14 in., max. 18 in. Flying Gurnards – Dactylopteridae
ID: **Huge, fanlike pectoral fins that often have brilliant, iridescent blue line and dot markings.** Body shades of gray to yellow-brown with white spots. Can pale or darken dramatically. Blunt snout. **RANGE:** Common to uncommon Caribbean; uncommon to rare Bahamas, S. Florida.

BANDTAIL SEAROBIN *Prionotus ophryas*
SIZE: 4-8 in., max. 1 ft. Searobins – Triglidae
ID: **Three reddish brown bars on tail.** Mottled and spotted, gray to reddish brown often with bars and bands. Large head with tapered snout. Pectoral fins long, and fanlike when extended. Inhabit shallow seagrass, sand and rubble. **RANGE:** Uncommon Caribbean, Bahamas, S. Florida.

BLUESPOTTED SEAROBIN *Prionotus roseus*
SIZE: 4-6 in., max. 8 in. Searobins – Triglidae
ID: **Pectoral fins extend to middle of second dorsal fin; brown with rows of bright blue spots that tend to form bands toward outer edge.** Light brown with spots. Dark bands on tail. **RANGE:** Uncommon Florida and Caribbean.

LEOPARD SEAROBIN *Prionotus scitulus*
SIZE: 4-7 in., max. 14 in. Searobins – Triglidae
ID: **Body and fins covered with leopardlike reddish brown spots; three or four dusky bands extend forward at a diagonal from back on to body.** Light brown. **RANGE:** Uncommon Florida and Caribbean.

REDSPOTTED HAWKFISH
Amblycirrhitus pinos
Hawkfishes – Cirrhitidae
SIZE: 2-3½ in., max. 4 in.
ID: **"Tassels" on tips of dorsal fin spines.** Red spots over head, upper body and dorsal fin. Brown bars over whitish background; fins (except dorsal) white to clear. Prefer coral reefs. Perch on bottom, and occasionally flit about for short distances. Wary; move to new perch when closely approached. Only member of hawkfish family in the Atlantic. **RANGE:** Common to occasional Caribbean, Bahamas, S. Florida.

SAND DIVER
Synodus intermedius
Lizardfishes – Synodontidae
SIZE: 4-14 in., max. 18 in.
ID: Dark spot at upper end of gill cover. Markings highly variable. Reddish brown bars across back. Often have thin yellow-gold and/or blue stripes. Can pale or darken quickly to blend with background. Diamond-shaped markings on side often join bars on back. **RANGE:** Common to occasional Caribbean, Bahamas, S. Florida.

INSHORE LIZARDFISH *Synodus foetens*
SIZE: 8-14 in., max. 18 in. Lizardfishes – Synodontidae
ID: Eight diamond to round markings with pale centers on sides that are separated from other markings. Gray to brown to greenish brown. Bar or saddle markings on back. Can pale or darken. Inhabit sand and silt in depths less than 25 ft. **RANGE:** Uncommon Caribbean, Bahamas, S. Florida.

BLUESTRIPE LIZARDFISH *Synodus saurus*
SIZE: 4-7 in., max. 12 in. Lizardfishes – Synodontidae
ID: Thin blue to turquoise stripes extend down upper body. Dark bars across back. Often show diamond-shaped patches on sides. Can pale or darken. Inhabit sand usually less than 12 ft. **RANGE:** Uncommon Bahamas; rare Caribbean; not reported S. Florida.

RED LIZARDFISH *Synodus synodus*
SIZE: 4-7 in., max. 13 in. Lizardfishes – Synodontidae
ID: Tiny black spot just behind tip of snout. Reddish brown to tan; may have bluish highlights. Can pale or darken or change bar pattern to blend with background; midline area darkens to form stripe. **RANGE:** Occasional eastern Caribbean; uncommon Bahamas, S. Florida.

SNAKEFISH *Trachinocephalus myops*
SIZE: 4-12 in., max. 15 in. Lizardfishes – Synodontidae
ID: Short, blunt snout with upturned mouth. Alternating stripes of pale blue and gold with narrow black borders run length of body; dusky wide bars on back. Short, dark diagonal streak at upper end of gill cover. **RANGE:** Occasional to uncommon Caribbean, Bahamas, S. Florida.

105

Frogfishes

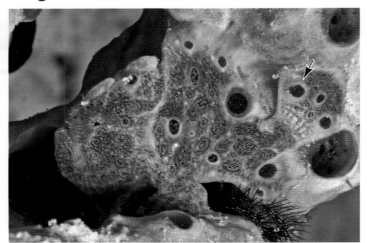

LONGLURE FROGFISH
Antennarius multiocellatus
Frogfishes – Antennariidae
SIZE: 3-5 in., max. 8 in.
ID: **Three spots on tail can usually be observed.** Often several occelated spots on body and fins. Large variety of color phases, including shades of deep red, pink, orange, yellow, green, black, tan and white. **RANGE:** Occasional Caribbean, S. Florida; rare Bahamas. Most commonly sighted frogfish in the Caribbean.

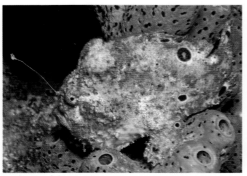

Longlure Frogfish – Variation
ID: Can change color, pale or darken over a period of days to weeks to match background. Long, whitish translucent filament, on the tip of a thin banded rod used to attract prey. Lie-in-wait predators perch on reef tops, often on sponges, typically blending into background.

Longlure Frogfish – Variation
ID: The photo [above] with three individuals demonstrates how well frogfish can blend into their surroundings. Usually solitary except when reproductively active. Females typically at least twice as large as males. Gravid females [upper left in photo], obviously swollen with eggs, attract courting males that remain nearby until spawning shortly after sunset.

STRIATED FROGFISH
Antennarius striatus
Frogfishes – Antennariidae
SIZE: 3-5 in., max. 7 in.
ID: **Irregular dark line and spot markings on head, body and fins.** Background color can vary from white to tan to almost black. The species' distinctive large, wormlike lure can be seen folded back resting between 1st and 2nd dorsal fin rays. Numerous skin filaments. **RANGE:** Occasional southeastern Caribbean; uncommon balance of Caribbean, S. Florida; rare Bahamas.

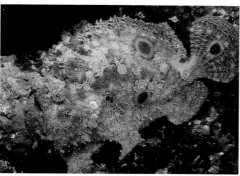

OCELLATED FROGFISH *Fowlerichthys ocellatus*

SIZE: 4-8 in., max. 15 in. Frogfishes – Antennariidae

ID: Three large, ocellated spots with dark centers on dorsal fin, midbody, and tail. Highly variable markings and colors. **RANGE:** Uncommon Caribbean, S. Florida; rare Bahamas.

Ocellated Frogfish – Variation

ID: Uniformly colored to heavily blotched and mottled. Colors and patterns are changeable over a period of days or weeks to blend with background.

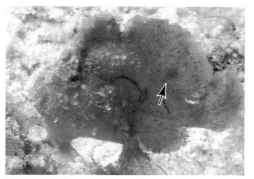

DWARF FROGFISH *Antennarius pauciradiatus*

SIZE: 1/2-3/4 in., max. 1 1/2 in. Frogfishes – Antennariidae

ID: Tiny. **Spot on base of 2nd dorsal fin toward rear of fin, which is usually dark, occasionally ocellated and uncommonly pale.** Yellowish tan to pale yellow to orange. **RANGE:** Rare S. Florida, Bahamas and Caribbean.

Dwarf Frogfish – Variation

ID: Yellow color variation with whitish spot on base of second dorsal fin.. Occasionally display other large spots or smudges.

SARGASSUMFISH

Histrio histrio

Frogfishes – Antennariidae

SIZE: 1 1/2-4 1/2 in., max. 8 in.

ID: Resemble *Sargassum* weed. Inhabit floating rafts of *Sargassum* weed (a free-floating algae that drifts on surface in open water). A variety of colors including brown, olive and yellow in patterns that blend with *Sargassum*. Large mouth. Numerous fleshy tabs on body. **RANGE:** Common in floats of *Sargassum* Caribbean, Bahamas, S. Florida.

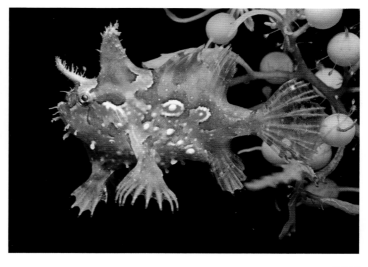

LONGSNOUT SEAHORSE *Hippocampus reidi*
SIZE: 2¹/₂-4 in., max. 6 in. Pipefishes & Seahorses – Syngnathidae
ID: Usually have small black spots over head and body. Colors vary from yellow to reddish orange, brown, white or black; may be two-toned. **RANGE:** Uncommon Caribbean, Bahamas, S. Florida.

Longsnout Seahorse – Variation
ID: Curl base of tail around branches of gorgonians, seagrass or other holdfasts. Occasionally float free over seagrass or reefs, and in *Sargassum.*

LINED SEAHORSE *Hippocampus erectus*
SIZE: 2-4 in., max. 6 in. Pipefishes & Seahorses – Syngnathidae
ID: Numerous lines on head and often down neck and back. Vary from reddish orange to brown or even black. Markings also vary. **RANGE:** Occasional southeastern Caribbean; rare Bahamas, S. Florida.

Lined Seahorse – Variation
ID: Often develop fleshy tabs and appendages when associated with algae habitats.

PIPEHORSE
Acentronura dendritica
Pipefishes & Seahorses – Syngnathidae
SIZE: 1-2 in., max. 3 in.
ID: Intermediate in form between seahorse and pipefish. Trumpet-like snout and small mouth; head slightly cocked. Body varies from whitish, translucent and blotched to uniformly dark overall. Small tail fin on curled base of tail. Clusters of fleshy tabs (papillae) on body. Considered pelagic, drift in open water or in floats of *Sargassum;* occasionally in seagrass beds and reefs, usually in clumps of algae. **RANGE:** Rare Caribbean, Bahamas, S. Florida.

HARLEQUIN PIPEFISH
Halicampus ensenadae
Pipefishes & Seahorses –
Syngnathidae
SIZE: 5-8 in., max. 9 in.
ID: Bold, alternating bands of brown and yellow. Trumpetlike snout and small mouth. Long, snakelike body. Dorsal fin clear. Move about the bottom, swimming through small holes, tunnels and recesses in reefs. Also inhabit grass and algae. Swim under and through tangles of vegetation and debris. **RANGE:** Occasional to rare Caribbean, Bahamas, S. Florida.

SHORTFIN PIPEFISH *Cosmocampus elucens*
SIZE: 3-5 in., max. 6 in. Pipefishes & Seahorses – Syngnathidae
ID: Two short, dark lines extend from rear of eye. Vary from dark brown to lavender. Long, slender snout. Long, snakelike body. Numerous pale body bands. **RANGE:** Rare Caribbean, Bahamas, S. Florida.

WHITENOSE PIPEFISH *Cosmocampus albirostris*
SIZE: 4-6 in., max. 8 in. Pipefishes & Seahorses – Syngnathidae
ID: White or unpigmented snout. Shades of brown, occasionally banded. Trumpetlike snout and small mouth. Long, snakelike body. **RANGE:** Occasional Caribbean, Bahamas, S. Florida.

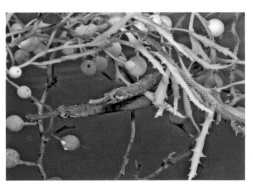

SARGASSUM PIPEFISH *Syngnathus pelagicus*
SIZE: 4-6 in., max. 8 in. Pipefishes & Seahorses – Syngnathidae
ID: Exclusively inhabit floats of *Sargassum* weed. White to pale shades of tan with brown bar, spot and ring markings. Long snakelike body. **RANGE:** Common to occasional Caribbean, Bahamas, S. Florida.

PEARLFISH *Carapus bermudensis*
SIZE: 3-6 in, max. 8 in. Pearlfishes – Carapidae
ID: Long translucent to transparent body tapers to a tail-less point. Pearly silver head. Lack fins except for a pectoral fin and a long transparent anal fin that begins just behind head. Nocturnal; retreat into the anus of sea cucumbers during the day. **RANGE:** Occasional Caribbean, Bahamas, S. Florida.

Odd-Shaped Swimmers
Trumpetfishes – Boxfishes
Triggerfishes & Filefishes
Drums & Croakers – Others

This ID Group consists of swimming fishes that do not have a typical fishlike shape.

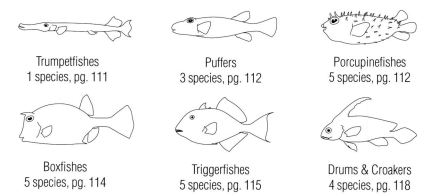

Trumpetfishes
1 species, pg. 111

Puffers
3 species, pg. 112

Porcupinefishes
5 species, pg. 112

Boxfishes
5 species, pg. 114

Triggerfishes
5 species, pg. 115

Drums & Croakers
4 species, pg. 118

Trumpetfishes, Aulostomidae – Trumpetfishes, with only a single family member in the Caribbean, are the most entertaining piscivores (predators that eat fish) on the reef. Their long, thin bodies scarcely cast shadows as the solitary hunters weave their way through bottom structures in search of prey. They disguise their presence by aligning their bodies with elongate structures such as branching gorgonians and mooring lines, and regularly shadow-feed with foraging fishes.

Puffers, Tetraodontidae – Puffers have the unique ability to draw in water to greatly inflate their bodies as a defense. Their fused teeth and powerful jaws are used to crush hard-shelled invertebrates.

Porcupinefishes, Diodontidae – Porcupinefishes have either long spines, which become erect when the fish inflates, or spines that are fixed in the erect position.

Triggerfishes, Balistidae – Triggerfishes and closely related filefishes, are similar in appearance. Members of both families are laterally compressed fishes with long first dorsal spines that can be raised or lowered. Triggerfishes have a more stout front dorsal spine, which can be locked in place, and crescent tails. The front dorsal spines of filefishes are long and slender and their tails are broom-shaped.

Boxfishes, Ostraciidae – Boxfishes are protected by a triangular, bony box of armor. They have small protrusible mouths and broomlike tails. They are divided into two groups: cowfishes, which have a sharp spine just above each eye; and trunkfishes, which lack these spines.

Drums & Croakers, Sciaenidae – The common name of these fishes is derived from their ability to vibrate muscles surrounding their swim bladders to produce a low-pitched, resonant sound. Reef-dwelling drums, especially juveniles, have unusually elongate foredorsal fins, making them quite striking. All are similarly patterned in white and black, but are easily distinguished.

Odd-Shaped Swimmers

ATLANTIC TRUMPETFISH
Aulostomus maculatus
Trumpetfishes – Aulostomidae
SIZE: 1½-2½ ft., max. 3 ft.

ID: Long, thin body. **Elongate trumpetlike mouth.** Three color variations: purplish [right], yellow and brown [below]. Do not change colors but can quickly pale or darken and frequently display bars and vague mottled pattern for camouflage. Often drift in vertical (feeding) position, head down, paralleling stalks of sea rods. Position their bodies against elongate structures such as mooring lines to help blend with background. **RANGE:** Common Caribbean, Bahamas, S. Florida.

Trumpetfish – Yellow Variation
ID: Active predators that often disguise their presence by aligning their bodies just above large fishes (behavior known as shadow feeding). Each variation shadow feeds with similar colored host. With Spanish Hogfish [above]. Purple variation often join aggregations of algae-feeding Blue Tang.

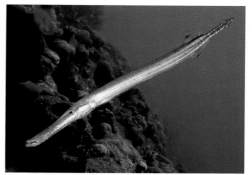

Trumpetfish – Brown Variation
ID: The most common of the three color variations.

BLUESPOTTED CORNETFISH
Fistularia tabacaria
Cornetfishes – Fistulariidae
SIZE: 2-4 ft., max. 6 ft.

ID: Long, extremely thin body. **Elongate tail filament.** Brownish gray to greenish brown, with blue dashes and spots. Snout and mouth shaped like a cornet. (Body length does not include tail filament.) Swim just above shallow beds of seagrass and near patch reefs. Occasionally found on deeper reefs. **RANGE:** Occasional southern and eastern Caribbean; uncommon northern Caribbean, Bahamas, S. Florida.

Puffers – Porcupinefishes

SHARPNOSE PUFFER
Canthigaster rostrata
Puffers – Tetraodontidae
SIZE: 2-3½ in., max. 4½ in.
ID: White to pale yellowish gold tail with dark borders. Dark olive-brown upper body, white to yellowish gold below with numerous blue dots; blue line markings around mouth, radiating from eyes and on base of tail. **RANGE:** Common to occasional Caribbean, Bahamas, S. Florida.

BANDTAIL PUFFER   *Sphoeroides spengleri*
SIZE: 4-7 in., max. 1 ft.   Puffers – Tetraodontidae
ID: Row of dark blotches from mouth to tail. Olive-brown; speckled upper body, white underside; two dark bands on tail. Pale or darken to blend with background. Inhabit shallow sand flats with seagrass. **RANGE:** Occasional Caribbean, Bahamas, S. Florida.

CHECKERED PUFFER   *Sphoeroides testudineus*
SIZE: 4-7 in., max. 1 ft.   Puffers – Tetraodontidae
ID: Polygon-shaped patches on back and sides are large and numerous, and range from brown to olive or gray. Tan to pale yellowish brown undercolor. Black spots on sides and cheeks. Inhabit shallow bays, inlets with seagrass. **RANGE:** Uncommon Caribbean, Bahamas, S. Florida.

BALLOONFISH
Diodon holocanthus
Porcupinefishes – Diodontidae
SIZE: 8-14 in., max. 20 in.
ID: Long spines on head. Olive to brown. Dusky band runs from eye to eye; may have dusky blotches or bands on back. Iris is yellow; pupil has iridescent blue-green speckling. Small dark spots on body; no spots on fins. Spines usually lowered, but may become erect without inflating body. **RANGE:** Occasional Caribbean, Bahamas, S. Florida.

PORCUPINEFISH
Diodon hystrix

Porcupinefishes – Diodontidae

SIZE: 1-2 ft., max. 3 ft.

ID: The largest member of the family. **Small, dark spots cover entire body and on fins.** Spines usually lie flat against the body, but may be raised when threatened. Olive to brown back, shading to white on belly. Can pale or darken. **RANGE:** Occasional Caribbean, Bahamas, S. Florida.

SPOTTED BURRFISH   *Chilomycterus reticulatus*

SIZE: 8-12 in., max. 14 in.   Porcupinefishes – Diodontidae

ID: Black spots on body and all fins. Upper body uneven shades of brown; may display large dark patches; belly white. Triangular spines are always erect. **RANGE:** Uncommon to rare Caribbean, S. Florida; not reported Bahamas.

WEB BURRFISH   *Chilomycterus antillarum*

SIZE: 6-10 in., max. 1 ft.   Porcupinefishes – Diodontidae

ID: Reticulated pattern on back and sides. Light to dark brown. Three to four large black spots on body. Iris is yellow-gold; pupil has iridescent blue-green specks. Spines always erect. **RANGE:** Occasional southern Caribbean; uncommon to rare northern Caribbean, Bahamas, S. Florida.

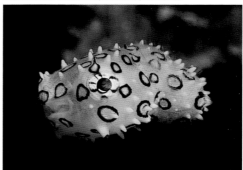

BRIDLED BURRFISH   *Chilomycterus antennatus*

SIZE: 6-10 in., max. 1 ft.   Porcupinefishes – Diodontidae

ID: Dark patch above each pectoral fin and another centered on rear body. Olive to yellowish brown. Iris is gold with circle of black dots; pupil has iridescent blue-green specks. Spines always erect. **RANGE:** Occasional northwestern Caribbean; uncommon to rare balance of range.

Bridled Burrfish – Post-larval Juvenile   **SIZE:** Less than ³/₄ in.

ID: Bright yellow with white spots ringed with black covering body.

Boxfishes – Triggerfishes

SCRAWLED COWFISH *Acanthostracion quadricornis*
SIZE: 8-15 in., max. 18 in. Boxfishes – Ostraciidae
ID: Scrawled pattern of bluish markings cover body. A sharp spine above each eye (distinguishes cowfishes from trunkfishes). Blue-green to yellow. Can darken, pale and change color. Two spines in front of anal fin. **RANGE:** Common S. Florida; occasional to uncommon Caribbean, Bahamas.

HONEYCOMB COWFISH *Acanthostracion polygonius*
SIZE: 7-15 in., max. 18 in. Boxfishes – Ostraciidae
ID: Honeycomb pattern on body. A sharp spine above each eye. Vary from shades of blue to green to yellow. Reticulated or scrawled design on head. Can darken or pale and change color. Two sharp spines in front of anal fin. **RANGE:** Occasional Caribbean, Bahamas, S. Florida.

TRUNKFISH *Lactophrys trigonus*
SIZE: 12-17 in., max. 19 in. Boxfishes – Ostraciidae
ID: Obvious hump on back. Vary greatly in shades of olive, green, yellow-brown, brown, blue-gray and gray. Can change color and display white spots on upper body and dark blotch markings. Base of tail long; two spines in front of anal fin. **RANGE:** Uncommon Caribbean, Bahamas, S. Florida.

SPOTTED TRUNKFISH *Lactophrys bicaudalis*
SIZE: 6-12 in., max. 16 in. Boxfishes – Ostraciidae
ID: White covered with black spots, including tail. Two sharp spines in front of anal fin (no spines above eyes). **RANGE:** Occasional to uncommon Caribbean, Bahamas, S. Florida.

SMOOTH TRUNKFISH *Lactophrys triqueter*
SIZE: 6-10 in., max. 1 ft. Boxfishes – Ostraciidae
ID: Only family member lacking spines either above the eye or near anal fin. Dark body covered with irregular white spots. Area of pale honeycomb markings on central body. **RANGE:** Common Caribbean, Bahamas, S. Florida.

Smooth Trunkfish – Post-larval Juvenile **SIZE:** ¼ in.
ID: Tiny size. Dark body covered with large white to pale yellow spots. As they mature develop honeycomb markings at midbody.

QUEEN TRIGGERFISH
Balistes vetula
Triggerfishes – Balistidae
SIZE: 8-16 in., max. 2 ft.
ID: Streaming tips on rear dorsal and tail fins. Body color in various shades of purple, blue, turquoise and green; lower half of head yellow or yellowish with two blue stripes. Dark lines radiate from around eye. Can pale or darken dramatically. **RANGE:** Common to occasional Caribbean, Bahamas, S. Florida.

GRAY TRIGGERFISH   *Balistes capriscus*
SIZE: 5-9 in. max. 1 ft.   Triggerfishes – Balistidae
ID: Blue spots and line markings on upper body and fins. Color varies from light gray to olive-gray to yellowish brown. Often have white dots and lines on lower body and fins. May have faint, broad bars or blotches on upper body. **RANGE:** Occasional S. Florida; rare Caribbean, Bahamas.

OCEAN TRIGGERFISH   *Canthidermis sufflamen*
SIZE: 10-18 in., max. 2 ft.   Triggerfishes – Balistidae
ID: Uniformly gray. **Black blotch at base of pectoral fin.** Vary from gray to grayish brown. Can pale or darken dramatically. **RANGE:** Occasional Caribbean, Bahamas, S. Florida.

SARGASSUM TRIGGERFISH   *Xanthichthys ringens*
SIZE: 5-8 in., max. 10 in.   Triggerfishes – Balistidae
ID: Three dark lines on cheek. Dashes form thin stripes on body. Vary from bluish gray to brownish gray. White dot just forward of eye, with white crescent bordering upper eye. Red to orange borders on tail. Usually below 80 ft. **RANGE:** Occasional Caribbean; uncommon Bahamas, S. Florida.

BLACK DURGON   *Melichthys niger*
SIZE: 6-12 in., max. 16 in.   Triggerfishes – Balistidae
ID: Blue-back body. **Pale blue lines run along base of dorsal and anal fins.** Blue and gold patches on head. Scales have pale diamond-shaped outline. Can change color, and pale or darken. Feed on plankton in open water along outer reefs. **RANGE:** Common to occasional Caribbean, Bahamas, S. Florida.

Filefishes

SCRAWLED FILEFISH
Aluterus scriptus
Filefishes – Monacanthidae
SIZE: 1-2½ ft., max. 3 ft.
ID: Covered with blue to blue-green spots, irregular lines and black dots. Elongate body with long, broomlike tail. Vary from pale gray or tan to dark olive-brown. Can darken or pale. Tail often closed and limp. **RANGE:** Occasional Caribbean, Bahamas, S. Florida.

UNICORN FILEFISH   *Aluterus monoceros*
SIZE: 8-18 in., max. 2 ft.   Filefishes – Monacanthidae
ID: Profile concave below small mouth. Gray to brown or silver with widely scattered brown spots; occasionally mottled; large adults typically silver [pictured]. Long tail base. **RANGE:** Rare Caribbean, Bahamas, S. Florida.

ORANGE FILEFISH   *Aluterus schoepfii*
SIZE: 10-18 in., max. 20 in.   Filefishes – Monacanthidae
ID: Body covered with orange dots. Extremely thin with long tail base. Pale silvery gray to dark gray, orange or orangish brown; often display large, dark areas or blotches. Can pale or darken. Often inhabit areas with seagrass. **RANGE:** Uncommon to rare Bahamas, S. Florida; rare Caribbean.

WHITESPOTTED FILEFISH   *Cantherhines macrocerus*
SIZE: 10-15 in., max. 18 in.   Filefishes – Monacanthidae
ID: Noticeably extended belly appendage. Upper body shades of gray to olive or brown with brown to orange below. Snout whitish; dorsal and anal fins are translucent yellow; tail dark. White spotted phase [pictured]. **RANGE:** Common to occasional Caribbean, Bahamas; Uncommon S. Florida.

Whitespotted Filefish – Orange Phase
ID: Often do not display white spots. Typically orange to gold with dark back.

ORANGESPOTTED FILEFISH *Cantherhines pullus*
SIZE: 4-7 in., max. 8½ in.   Filefishes – Monacanthidae
ID: White spot on upper base of tail. Typically have wide, dark brown stripes and narrow, dull yellow stripes that converge near tail base. Can change to solid brown, darken or pale. Orangish spots cover body. **RANGE:** Common Caribbean, S. Florida; uncommon Bahamas.

PLANEHEAD FILEFISH *Stephanolepis hispidus*
SIZE: 4-8 in., max. 10 in.   Filefishes – Monacanthidae
ID: Thicker body than most family members and nearly straight snout and nape profile. Usually blotched in variable shades of tan to brown or gray, occasionally greenish. **RANGE:** Occasional S. Florida; uncommon Caribbean, Bahamas.

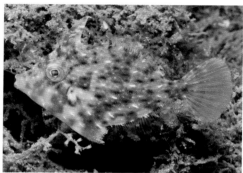

FRINGED FILEFISH *Monacanthus ciliatus*
SIZE: 3-5 in., max. 8 in.   Filefishes – Monacanthidae
ID: Base of dorsal fin has steep hump and tail often banded. Variable shades of brown to reddish brown, yellow-brown, green or gray; usually have numerous dark and white speckles, spots and blotches. Often inhabit seagrass. **RANGE:** Uncommon Caribbean, Bahamas, S. Florida.

PYGMY FILEFISH *Stephanolepis setifer*
SIZE: 2-4 in., max. 7½ in.   Filefishes – Monacanthidae
ID: Vague, incomplete body stripes formed by dashes and spots. Usually variably blotched and spotted, in shades of tan to yellow-brown or brown, but can change color to match surroundings. Often inhabit floats of *Sargassum* weed. **RANGE:** Uncommon Caribbean, Bahamas, S. Florida.

SLENDER FILEFISH *Monacanthus tuckeri*
SIZE: 2-3½ in., max. 4 in.   Filefishes – Monacanthidae
ID: Variable shades of reddish brown to yellow-brown, brown or gray; upper body usually darker. Often display reticulated pattern. Often exhibit fleshy tabs on head and body. Inhabit gorgonian colonies and other densely branching structures. **RANGE:** Occasional Caribbean, Bahamas, S. Florida.

Slender Filefish – Phase
ID: Can change color, pale or darken dramatically to blend with background; reticulated markings may become indistinct especially when outside protective branches. Large dewlap (extendible belly appendage) usually has yellowish edge with submarginal blue line.

GLASSY SWEEPER *Pempheris schomburgkii*
SIZE: 3-5 in., max. 6 in. Sweepers – Pempheridae
ID: Shiny copper-colored, hatchet-shaped body. **Dark band at base of anal fin.** Large eyes and thin body. Congregate in small groups to large schools under ledges and inside caves. Nocturnal feeders. **RANGE:** Common to occasional Caribbean, Bahamas, S. Florida.

SHORTFIN SWEEPER *Pempheris poeyi*
SIZE: 1-3 in., max. 4 in. Sweepers – Pempheridae
ID: Shiny unmarked, silvery, hatchet-shaped body. Tend to inhabit caves and crevices of inshore surge zones. Seldom deeper than 15 ft. Nocturnal feeders. **RANGE:** Uncommon Caribbean, Bahamas, S. Florida.

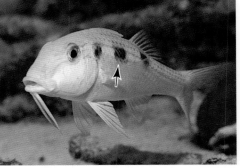

YELLOW GOATFISH *Mulloidichthys martinicus*
SIZE: 6-12 in., max. 15½ in. Goatfishes – Mullidae
ID: **White with yellow tail and midbody stripe.** (Resemble Yellowtail Snapper.) Two barbles (whiskers) on chin (family trademark). Fins, other than tail, may be white or yellowish. Feed in sand, often with other species; hover in small to large aggregations. **RANGE:** Common Caribbean, Bahamas, S. Florida.

SPOTTED GOATFISH *Pseudupeneus maculatus*
SIZE: 5-8 in., max. 11 in. Goatfishes – Mullidae
ID: **White with a row of three dark, rectangular body blotches.** Two chemosensory barbles (whiskers) on chin (family trademark), used to locate prey beneath sand. When resting on bottom display a reddish mottled pattern. **RANGE:** Common Caribbean, Bahamas, S. Florida.

SAND TILEFISH *Malacanthus plumieri*
SIZE: 1-1½ ft., max. 2 ft. Tilefishes – Malacanthidae
ID: **Elongate body with long undulating dorsal and anal fins in shades of white.** Crescent tail with dark blotch and yellow highlights. Hover over sand, often near large rubble burrows. **RANGE:** Common to occasional Caribbean, Bahamas, S. Florida.

REEF CROAKER *Odontoscion dentex*
SIZE: 4-7½ in., max. 1 ft. Drums & Croakers – Sciaenidae
ID: **Black spot at base of pectoral fin.** Pale reddish brown to gray with silvery sheen. Large eyes and somewhat elongate body. Nocturnal feeder; reclusive during day. **RANGE:** Occasional S. Florida; uncommon eastern Caribbean; rare to absent balance of Caribbean; not reported Bahamas.

SPOTTED DRUM *Equetus punctatus*
SIZE: 6-9 in., max. 11 in. Drums & Croakers – Sciaenidae
ID: Rear dorsal and tail fins black with white spots. Front dorsal fin long. Black and white bars on head, and multiple stripes on body. Nocturnal feeder, hover near or inside reef recesses during day. **RANGE:** Occasional Caribbean, Bahamas, S. Florida.

Spotted Drum – Juvenile **SIZE:** ³/₄ -1 ¹/₂ in.
ID: Black spot on nose. (Similar Jackknife Fish [next] has vertical black dash on nose.) Extremely long dorsal fin. Black and white bars on head and long black stripe from dorsal fin to tail.

HIGHHAT *Pareques acuminatus*
SIZE: 5-8 in., max. 9 in. Drums & Croakers – Sciaenidae
ID: Black and white striped body (uncommonly have dark variation). Elongate dark foredorsal fin edged in white; all other fins dark. Nocturnal feeder, hover near or inside reef recesses during day. **RANGE:** Common S. Florida; occasional Caribbean, Bahamas.

Highhat – Juvenile **SIZE:** ³/₄ -1 ¹/₂ in.
ID: Young juveniles have a black curving band extending from nape around foredorsal fin, joining behind and under the transparent soft dorsal fin.

JACKKNIFE FISH *Equetus lanceolatus*
SIZE: 5-8 in., max. 9 in. Drums & Croakers – Sciaenidae
ID: Fins without spots. Yellowish cream with single black band from top of front dorsal fin along midbody line to tip of tail. Elongate, pointed front dorsal fin. Nocturnal feeder. **RANGE:** Occasional to uncommon Bahamas, S. Florida; rare Caribbean. Juveniles more commonly sighted than adults.

Jackknife Fish – Juvenile **SIZE:** 1¹/₂ -3 in.
ID: Black markings of young are are edged with yellow-gold. **Vertical black dash on nose.** (Similar Spotted Drum [previous] has black dot on nose.) With maturity, yellow fades to yellowish white.

BLACK BROTULA *Stygnobrotula latebricola*
SIZE: 1¹/₂-2¹/₂ in., max. 3 in. Viviparous Brotulas – Bythitidae
ID: Brownish to black elongate body becoming ribbonlike toward rear. Continuous dorsal and anal fins end with pointed tail. Reclusive; inhabit crevices, recesses and caves in reefs. Often in pairs. **RANGE:** Occasional southern Caribbean; uncommon balance of Caribbean, Bahamas, S. Florida.

ATLANTIC TRIPLETAIL *Lobotes surinamensis*
SIZE: 1¹/₂-2¹/₂ ft., max. 3¹/₂ ft. Tripletails – Lobotidae
ID: Rear dorsal and anal fins large. Lightly mottled; vary from cream to yellow-brown, greenish brown, gray and black. Float on their sides near surface under *Sargassum*, docks, buoys and anchored boats. **RANGE:** Uncommon Caribbean, Bahamas, S. Florida.

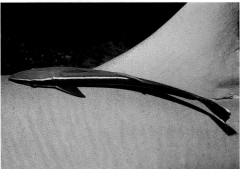

OCEAN SUNFISH *Mola mola*
SIZE: 3-7 ft., max. 10 ft. Molas – Molidae
ID: Large size and unique shape. Broad oval body. Silver to gray or gray-brown gradating to whitish belly. Long dorsal and anal fins. Oceanic; occasionally near deep reefs to be cleaned. Often tip of dorsal fin breaks surface; also bask at the surface. **RANGE:** Rare Caribbean, Bahamas, S. Florida.

SHARKSUCKER *Echeneis naucrates*
SIZE: 10-18 in., max. 3¹/₂ ft. Remoras – Echeneidae
ID: Thin white borders on dark tail. Black midbody stripe bordered with white stripes; thin white border on dorsal and anal fins. Foredorsal fin modified to form a suction disc used for attaching to hosts such as sharks, rays, large fish and turtles. **RANGE:** Occasional Caribbean, Bahamas, S. Florida.

WHITEFIN SHARKSUCKER *Echeneis neucratoides*
SIZE: 10-18 in., max. 2¹/₂ ft. Remoras – Echeneidae
ID: Wide white borders on dark tail base. Black midbody stripe bordered with wide white stripes; white border on dorsal and anal fins. Foredorsal fin modified to form a suction disc used for attaching to hosts such as sharks, rays, large fish and turtles. **RANGE:** Uncommon Caribbean, Bahamas, S. Florida.

REMORA *Remora remora*
SIZE: 8-15 in., max. 31 in. Remoras – Echeneidae
ID: Uniform coloration without distinctive markings, except for varying amounts of speckling. Attach to large free-swimming fishes, primarily sharks and mantas. **RANGE:** Uncommon Caribbean, Bahamas, S. Florida.

Eels
Morays – Conger Eels/Garden Eels – Snake Eels

This ID Group consists of fishes with long, snakelike bodies. They are generally found on the bottom in dark reef recesses, or in sand.

Morays
10 species, pg. 122

Conger Eels/ Garden Eels
3 species, pg. 124

Snake Eels
5 species, pg. 125

Morays, Muraenidae – Morays have no pectoral or ventral fins, and their dorsal, tail and anal fins form a single, long continuous fin that begins behind the head, encircles the tail and extends midway down the belly. Their heavy, scaleless bodies are coated with a clear film of protective mucus. During the day, most species are reclusive and tend to hide in dark recesses. Occasionally they are seen with their heads extending from holes. All are nocturnal foragers except for the Spotted Moray and Goldentail Moray, which feed during the day, often in association with a pack of small groupers and other fishes (a behavior known as nuclear hunting). Colors and markings make visual identification of most morays simple. Several species have the ability to change colors, becoming drab, mottled or pale. Morays constantly open and close their mouths, which is often perceived as a threat, but in reality is a behavior necessary to move water through their gills for respiration. They are not aggressive, although they can inflict a nasty bite if molested, and will swim off the bottom to approach divers in areas where fish feeding occurs.

Conger Eels/Garden Eels, Ophichthidae – The dorsal, anal and tail fins of conger eels are continuous, but unlike morays, they also have pectoral fins. Most species are thin and elongate, with dull colors and few markings. Because they live deep within recesses in the reef, they are rarely seen by divers. An exception are garden eels that live in colonies on open sand plains with their forebodies protruding and their backs arched as they nab bits of drifting zooplankton from the currents.

Snake Eels, Ophichthidae – Most snake eels are virtually without fins and strongly resemble snakes. In fact, when first encountered, uninformed divers think they have encountered a sea snake, although these reptiles do not inhabit the waters of the Tropical Western Atlantic. Many snake eels are shy and reclusive, hiding in dark recesses or burrowing beneath the sand during the day with their heads occasionally exposed. Others, such as the Sharptail Eels, forage in the open during daylight hours. The colors, patterns and sizes of spots are the primary keys for identification.

Morays

GREEN MORAY
Gymnothorax funebris

Morays – Muraenidae

SIZE: 3-5 ft., max. 8 ft.

ID: Uniform green to brown. Heavy body with no markings. Wide range of habitats, from murky bays to clearwater reefs. Hide during the day in recesses often with their heads extending from openings. Nocturnal; forage in open at night. Not aggressive, but will bite if they are molested; constantly open and close mouth, an action required for respiration, not a threat. **RANGE:** Occasional Caribbean, Bahamas, S. Florida.

SPOTTED MORAY   *Gymnothorax moringa*

SIZE: 1¹/₂-3 ft., max. 4 ft.   Morays – Muraenidae

ID: Speckling of dark spots and blotches cover body. Heavy to medium body. Pale undercolor from white to yellow. On occasion a reverse color pattern with dark background and light spots. Forage in the open during the day and night. **RANGE:** Common Caribbean; occasional Bahamas, S. Florida.

RETICULATE MORAY   *Muraena retifera*

SIZE: 8-18 in., max. 2 ft.   Morays – Muraenidae

ID: Dark spot around gill opening. Pale, often yellowish spots, or rosettes covering head and body. Dark brown undercolor. Medium body. Nostrils have tubular extensions. Forage in open at night. **RANGE:** Rare north coast of South America and offshore islands, S. Florida.

PURPLEMOUTH MORAY
Gymnothorax vicinus

Morays – Muraenidae

SIZE: 1¹/₂-3 ft., max. 4 ft.

ID: Yellow-gold eyes. Densely mottled in shades of brown over yellowish undercolor. Dark edge on dorsal fin. Inside of mouth lavender and purple. Forage in open at night. Inhabit shallow reefs and rocks in areas with clear water. **RANGE:** Uncommon Caribbean, Bahamas, S. Florida.

122

VIPER MORAY *Enchelycore nigricans*
SIZE: 1-2 ft., max. 2½ ft. Morays – Muraenidae
ID: **Jaws arched, with only tips making contact when closed; numerous sharp, pointed teeth visible.** Thin, dark brown to maroon body, often lightly mottled. Forage in open at night. Reclusive; retreat when approached. **RANGE:** Uncommon Caribbean, Bahamas, S. Florida.

CHESTNUT MORAY *Enchelycore carychroa*
SIZE: 8-10 in., max. 13 in. Morays – Muraenidae
ID: **Series of white spots along edges of jaws.** Thin reddish brown body. Black line markings in area of gill openings; white and black rings around eye. Jaws arched, with only tips making contact when closed; numerous sharp, pointed teeth. **RANGE:** Rare Caribbean, Bahamas, S. Florida.

GOLDENTAIL MORAY
Gymnothorax miliaris
Morays – Muraenidae
SIZE: 1-1½ ft., max. 2 ft.
ID: Shades of brown covered with small yellow spots (size of spots can vary considerably between individuals and, on rare occasions, can be reversed, with a yellow undercolor and brown spots, or a brown netlike pattern). Tip of tail yellow to gold on most individuals. Ring of yellow around pupil. Forage during day; prefer shallow to mid-range coral reefs. **RANGE:** Common to occasional Caribbean; occasional Bahamas, S. Florida.

Goldentail Moray – Variation
ID: Occasionally yellowish undercolor with dark netlike pattern.

Goldentail Moray – Variation
ID: In some cases an individual can be quite dark and without a golden tail.

CHAIN MORAY
Echidna catenata
Morays – Muraenidae
SIZE: 1-1½ ft., max. 2½ ft.

ID: Pale yellowish to bright yellow chainlike markings (pattern mimics dappled sunlight) on dark brown to black body. Yellow eyes. Prefer shallow, clearwater reefs and rocky shores. Hide during the day in recesses often with heads extended from openings. Forage at night in shallow water where they feed on crabs; occasionally in tidal pools. **RANGE:** Common to occasional eastern and southern Caribbean; occasional Bahamas and S. Florida; rare Cayman Is. and western Caribbean.

BROADBANDED MORAY   *Channomuraena vittata*
SIZE: 1½-4 ft., max. 5 ft.   Morays – Muraenidae
ID: Numerous wide, dark and pale bands ring body. Heavy body with dark reddish brown, dark gray or olive bands. Head enlarges abruptly behind short snout; small eye set forward; wrinkled skin on head and body. **RANGE:** Rare eastern Caribbean, Bahamas.

REDFACE MORAY   *Monopenchelys acuta*
SIZE: 3-5 in., max. 7 in.   Morays – Muraenidae
ID: Small size, not much larger than a soda straw, with orange head and dusky orange body. Reclusive; usually sighted within crevices between lobes of star coral, also inhabit areas of rubble. **RANGE:** Rare Caribbean, Bahamas.

BROWN GARDEN EEL   *Heteroconger longissimus*
SIZE: 8-15 in., max. 20 in. Conger Eels/Garden Eels – Congridae
ID: Brown to gray head and upper body. Often tiny orangish spots on thin body with pale belly and jutting lower jaw. Live in colonies on sand flats extending head and upper body from burrows to catch drifting plankton. **RANGE:** Common to occasional Caribbean, Bahamas, S. Florida.

YELLOW GARDEN EEL   *Heteroconger luteolus*
SIZE: 8-15 in., max. 20 in. Conger Eels/Garden Eels – Congridae
ID: Yellow back and white belly. Gather in small colonies on sand flats extending head and upper body from burrows. Continuously move in graceful, wavelike motions to catch drifting plankton. **RANGE:** Uncommon S. Florida.

MANYTOOTH CONGER *Conger triporiceps*
SIZE: 1-2½ ft., max. 3½ ft.   Conger Eels – Congridae
ID: Dark border on dorsal, tail and anal fins. Usually bluish gray to gray, occasionally shades of brown. Nocturnal; inhabit reefs and rubble areas. **RANGE:** Occasional to uncommon Bahamas, Caribbean (primarily near islands); rare S. Florida.

BLACKSPOTTED EEL *Quassiremus ascensionis*
SIZE: 1-2 ft., max. 2½ ft.   Snake Eels – Ophichthidae
ID: Large, diffuse rusty spots with dark to black centers on body. Tan to olive brown gradating to whitish belly. Network of small dark spots on head with paired white spots on snout. **RANGE:** Uncommon to rare Bahamas and eastern Caribbean. Not reported balance of Caribbean, S. Florida.

SHARPTAIL EEL *Myrichthys breviceps*
SIZE: 1-2½ ft., max. 3½ ft.   Snake Eels – Ophichthidae
ID: Large, diffuse, pale spots on body. Small yellow spots on head. Thin body. Often grayish, but can be olive to purplish brown. Body spots often have pale yellow centers. **RANGE:** Occasional to uncommon continental coasts of Caribbean, S. Florida; uncommon to rare Bahamas, Caribbean islands.

GOLDSPOTTED EEL *Myrichthys ocellatus*
SIZE: 1-2½ ft., max. 3½ ft.   Snake Eels – Ophichthidae
ID: Bright yellow-gold spots with diffuse black borders cover body and head. Thin body may have tan, yellow to green cast. Active at night; also seen during the day. **RANGE:** Occasional to uncommon Caribbean islands, Bahamas; uncommon to rare continental coasts of Caribbean, S. Florida.

SPOTTED SNAKE EEL *Ophichthus ophis*
SIZE: 1-2½ ft., max. 4 ft.   Snake Eels – Ophichthidae
ID: Broad, dark bar across top of head may extend down onto cheeks. Vary from white to gray, cream or tan; often have yellowish cast. Inhabit sand; often with only head and upper body exposed. **RANGE:** Uncommon eastern and southern; rare remainder of Caribbean, Bahamas, S. Florida.

SPOTTED SPOON-NOSE EEL *Echiophis intertinctus*
SIZE: 2-3 ft., max. 6 ft.   Snake Eels – Ophichthidae
ID: Short, pointed, V-shaped snout. Cream to pale yellowish; covered with numerous large, irregular spots on back and small spots on head. Inhabit sand; often with only head and upper body exposed. **RANGE:** Uncommon eastern and southern; rare remainder of Caribbean, Bahamas, S. Florida.

Sharks & Rays

Nurse Sharks – Pointed-Nose Sharks
Hammerhead Sharks – Rays

This ID Group consists of fishes whose skeletons are composed of cartilage rather than bone, and therefore commonly known as cartilaginous fishes. All have small, hard scales that give them a rough, sandpapery feel. Sharks and rays are classified into numerous families, which are often difficult to distinguish. Consequently, they will be discussed more by their general appearance rather than by family.

Nurse Sharks	Pointed-Nose Sharks	Hammerhead Sharks	Rays
1 species, pg.127	8 species, pg. 127	3 species, pg. 129	8 species, pg. 130

Nurse Sharks, Ginglymostomatidae – Nurse Shark, the lone family member in the Tropical Western Atlantic, are nocturnal bottom feeders that prey primarily on crustaceans, mollusks, and fishes, including stingrays. They are typically sighted during the day resting under the protection of reef ledges. Their long tail that can reach a quarter the length of their bodies is distinctive. Although they are easily approached and appear docile while at rest, these large animals can inflict a nasty bite if molested.

Pointed-Nose Sharks, Carcharhinidae & Lamnidae – Sharks with more-or-less pointed noses are represented by at least eight families in the Tropical Western Atlantic. Generally, they are rarely observed by divers and, when sighted, are extremely difficult to distinguish. Important clues for underwater identification are the general shape of the snout, placement of the dorsal fin in relation to the pectoral fin, and the shape and size of fins.

Hammerhead Sharks, Sphyrnidae – Hammerhead sharks are easily identified by their wide flattened heads that set their eyes far apart. It is believed that their head's unique shape helps to improve vision, electrical reception and hydrodynamics. Species can be determined by observing the shape of the head's leading edge. Family members are bottom feeders with disproportionately small mouths that dine on a variety of crustaceans, squids and fishes.

Rays – Rays are represented by ten families in the Tropical Western Atlantic. Their greatly enlarged pectoral fins, which give them a disclike shape, provide propulsion for swimming much like birds use their wings for flight. Members of eight families are bottom-dwellers. The most common families are guitarfishes, electric rays, skates and stingrays. All have mouths on the bottom of their heads. Electric rays are distinguished by their circular shape and thick, short tails. As the common family name implies, these fishes have the ability to discharge an electrical shock. Skates and stingrays generally have more pointed snouts and "wing-tips." Stingrays have sharp spines on their elongate tails, while skates do not. "Flying" rays — Eagle Rays and Mantas — spend most the time swimming. Eagle Rays regularly dig for mollusks in the open sand, whereas Mantas filter feed in open water.

WHALE SHARK
Rhincodon typus

Whale Sharks – Rhincodontidae

SIZE: 20-45 ft., max. 55 ft.

ID: Bold pattern of large, white spots cover body. Gray to gray-brown, fading to white below; thin whitish lines join spots on back. Three ridges run along sides from head to base of tail; first dorsal fin more than halfway back on body. World's largest fish. Considered oceanic. Occasionally cruise along walls and steep slopes. Feed on plankton, baitfish, tuna, squid and pelagic crustaceans that are sieved from the water. **RANGE:** Rare Caribbean, Bahamas, S. Florida.

NURSE SHARK
Ginglymostoma cirratum

SIZE: 5-9 ft., max. 14 ft. Nurse Sharks – Ginglymostomatidae

ID: Two barbels on upper lip of small mouth. Vary from gray to yellow-brown. Tail fin has no distinct lower lobe. In all habitats, from shallow water to outer reefs. Often lie on sand under ledges and overhangs. **RANGE:** Occasional Caribbean, Bahamas, S. Florida.

TIGER SHARK
Galeocerdo cuvier

Requiem Sharks – Carcharhinidae

SIZE: 7-12 ft., max. 24 ft.

ID: Dark bars and blotches on body. Bluish to brownish gray with pale belly. Short, broad snout; upper lobe of tail long. Cruise all waters; usually solitary. Voracious predator. Considered dangerous; can be aggressive, especially in the vicinity of spearfishing. **RANGE:** Rare Caribbean, Bahamas, S. Florida.

LEMON SHARK
Negaprion brevirostris

SIZE: 5-8 ft., max. 11 ft.   Requiem Sharks – Carcharhinidae

ID: Second dorsal fin nearly equal in size to first. Back commonly yellowish brown, but can be brown or gray. Upper lobe of tail much larger than lower. **RANGE:** Occasional S. Florida and continental waters to northern South America; uncommon Bahamas, Caribbean islands.

BULL SHARK
Carcharhinus leucas
Requiem Sharks – Carcharhinidae
SIZE: 6-9 ft., max. 12 ft.
ID: Heavy body with no markings on fins. Gray to brown with pale belly. Upper lobe of tail much larger than lower. Short snout and small eyes. Dorsal fin begins above mid-pectoral fin. Cruise inshore waters and reefs, occasionally form small groups. Considered dangerous, especially in the vicinity of spearfishing.
RANGE: Occasional S. Florida and continental waters to northern South America; rare islands of Caribbean, Bahamas.

ATLANTIC SHARPNOSE SHARK   *Rhizoprionodon terraenovae*
SIZE: 2-3 ft., max. 3¹/₂ ft.   Requiem Sharks – Carcharhinidae
ID: Long, flattened snout. Olive-gray to brown with pale belly. Often have a few scattered pale spots. Dorsal and tail fins may be edged in black. Second dorsal fin begins above middle of anal fin. Inhabit shallow coastal waters. **RANGE:** Uncommon Caribbean, Bahamas, S. Florida.

SILKY SHARK   *Carcharhinus falciformis*
SIZE: 5-7 ft., max. 10 ft.   Requiem Sharks – Carcharhinidae
ID: Ridge on back between first and second dorsal fins. Relatively slender. Silvery gray with white belly; dusky edge often on pectoral, second dorsal, anal and upper tail fins. Dorsal fin rounded, relatively small. Openwater species. **RANGE:** Uncommon Caribbean, Bahamas, S. Florida.

REEF SHARK   *Carcharhinus perezii*
SIZE: 5-8 ft., max. 10 ft.   Requiem Sharks – Carcharhinidae
ID: Inside tips of pectoral fins and tips of ventral fins, anal fins and lower lobe of tail are dusky. Heavy body silvery gray with white belly. Gill slits relatively small and start above plane of pectoral fin. Cruise reefs and shallows. **RANGE:** Occasional Caribbean, Bahamas, S. Florida.

BLACKTIP SHARK   *Carcharhinus limbatus*
SIZE: 5-6¹/₂ ft., max. 8¹/₂ ft.   Requiem Sharks – Carcharhinidae
ID: Silver white streak on flank. Anal fin pale to white. Black tips and edging may be indistinct, especially on first dorsal. Bluish silver-gray on back fading to white belly. Cruise reefs and shallows, occasionally in lagoons. **RANGE:** Uncommon Caribbean, Bahamas, S. Florida.

OCEANIC WHITETIP SHARK *Carcharhinus longimanus*
SIZE: 7-10 ft., max. 12 ft.   Requiem Sharks – Carcharhinidae
ID: Large rounded foredorsal fin with large white tip. Medium brown to gray brown upper body, yellowish white belly. Long pectoral fins, usually with white tips. Rounded snout. Pelagic; not over reefs. **RANGE:** Uncommon Caribbean, Bahamas, S. Florida.

SHORTFIN MAKO *Isurus oxyrinchus*
SIZE: 5-9 ft., max. 12½ ft.   Mackerel Sharks – Lamnidae
ID: Slender, conical snout. Large dorsal fin begins above and just behind pectoral fin. Lobes of tail nearly equal in size. Large black eyes. Front teeth slender and curved backwards. Oceanic, rarely over reefs. **RANGE:** Uncommon Caribbean, Bahamas, S. Florida.

SCALLOPED HAMMERHEAD
Sphyrna lewini

Hammerhead Sharks – Sphyrnidae
SIZE: 5-9 ft., max. 14 ft.
ID: Front edge of "hammer" curved and deeply scalloped. Rear edge of ventral fin straight. Gray with pale belly. First dorsal fin has rounded tip. Considered oceanic, though occasionally cruise reefs, walls and shallows; often in groups. **RANGE:** Uncommon Caribbean, Bahamas, S. Florida.

GREAT HAMMERHEAD *Sphyrna mokarran*
SIZE: 5-14 ft., max. 20 ft.   Hammerhead Sharks – Sphyrnidae
ID: Front edge of "hammer" slightly curved and not deeply scalloped. Rear edge of ventral fin curved. Gray with pale belly. First dorsal fin tall, pointed and curved toward rear; small eyes. Unpredictable, considered dangerous. **RANGE:** Rare Caribbean, Bahamas, S. Florida.

BONNETHEAD *Sphyrna tiburo*
SIZE: 3-4 ft., max. 5 ft.   Hammerhead Sharks – Sphyrnidae
ID: Small, with smooth "spade-shaped" head. Gray with pale belly. Inhabit shallow bays, sounds and estuaries. **RANGE:** Occasional continental waters to northern South America, western Bahamas and Cuba, S. Florida; not reported other Caribbean islands.

129

ATLANTIC GUITARFISH *Rhinobatos lentiginosus*
SIZE: 1-2 ft., max. 2½ ft.   Guitarfish – Rhinobatidae
ID: Head and pectoral fins form a triangular raylike forebody. Thick, tapered, sharklike rear body. Vary from gray to brown, with many pale spots. Have rectangular area on each side of pointed snout. **RANGE:** Uncommon S. Florida, Yucatan; not reported Bahamas, Caribbean islands.

ATLANTIC STINGRAY *Dasyatis sabina*
SIZE: 1-1½ ft., max. 2 ft.   Whiptail Stingrays – Dasyatidae
ID: Pointed snout and rounded "wing" tips. Tan to brown. Long thin tail. Smallest stingray in western Atlantic. **RANGE:** Common west coast of Florida and northern Gulf of Mexico; Occasional east coast of Florida.

SOUTHERN STINGRAY *Dasyatis americana*
SIZE: 3-4 ft., max. 5½ ft.   Whiptail Stingrays – Dasyatidae
ID: Snout and tips of "wings" pointed. Vary from brown to gray and black; belly white. Whiplike tail with one or two venomous spines at base. Size excludes tail. Lie on bottom, often covered with sand with only eyes protruding. **RANGE:** Common Caribbean; occasional Bahamas, S. Florida.

YELLOW STINGRAY *Urobatis jamaicensis*
SIZE: 8-12 in., max. 15 in.   Round Stingrays – Urolophidae
ID: Numerous spots. Snout and tips of "wings" rounded. Yellowish brown with numerous pale and dark spots and blotches; can change color and pale or darken. Stout tail with venomous spine near end. Size excludes tail. **RANGE:** Occasional S. Florida; uncommon Caribbean, Bahamas.

LESSER ELECTRIC RAY *Narcine bancroftii*
SIZE: 10-15 in., max. 18 in.   Electric Rays – Narcinidae
ID: Circular forebody and short tail with thick base and two dorsal fins of equal size. Shades of gray to brown. Color may be uniform or with dark blotches and circles. **RANGE:** Occasional southeastern and southern Caribbean; uncommon S. Florida; rare to absent Bahamas and balance of Caribbean.

CARIBBEAN TORPEDO *Torpedo andersoni*
SIZE: 9-12 in., max. 13 in. Torpedo Electric Rays – Torpedinidae
ID: Front of broad, circular forebody is squared. Tan with light brown blotches. Front edge of disc is scalloped. First dorsal fin is tall, and much larger than second. If touched, can deliver an electric shock. **RANGE:** Rare Caribbean, Bahamas, S. Florida.

SPOTTED EAGLE RAY
Aetobatus narinari
Eagle Rays – Myliobatidae
SIZE: 4-6½ ft., max. 8 ft.
ID: Numerous white spots and circular markings over dark back vary significantly between individuals. White belly. Pronounced head with flattened, tapered snout. Long, thin tail with one to five venomous spines at base. Occasionally cruise walls in schools. **RANGE:** Common to occasional Caribbean, Bahamas, S. Florida.

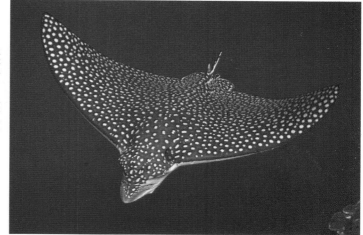

OCEANIC MANTA RAY
Mobula birostis
Devil Rays – Mobulidae
SIZE: 6-16 in., max. 27 ft.
ID: Large black mouth on leading edge of head. Dorsal surfaces black with white "shoulder" patches that form outline of a black "T". White ventral surface has various-size black spots behind gill slits; occasionally there are additional dark patches along trailing edges of the gill slits.
RANGE: Uncommon Florida, Bahamas, Caribbean; also circumtropical and subtropical.

CARIBBEAN MANTA RAY
Manta sp. cf. birostris
Devil Rays – Mobulidae
SIZE: 6-14 ft., max. 22 ft.
ID: Large white mouth on leading edge of head. Dark back, often with whitish patches on shoulder and, occasionally, other areas. White belly, can be grayish. Oceanic; cruise near surface, filtering plankton from water. Occasionally pass along walls and over outer reef lines. Easily confused with Devil Ray, *Mobula hypostoma*, which are smaller, not exceeding four feet in width, and typically cruise in large schools. Mouth located below leading edge of head; black back. **RANGE:** Uncommon Caribbean, Bahamas, S. Florida.

  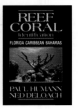
 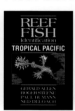 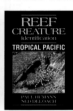   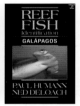